Christ's Prisoner

Christ's Prisoner

WALKING WITH JESUS
VOLUME THREE

*An Expository Commentary
based upon Paul's Letter to the Ephesians*

(CHAPTER THREE VERSES 1–21)

ROBERT B. CALLAHAN, SR.

RESOURCE *Publications* · Eugene, Oregon

CHRIST'S PRISONER
An Expository Commentary based upon Paul's Letter to the Ephesians
(Chapter Three Verses 1–21)

Copyright © 2011 Robert B. Callahan, Sr. All rights reserved. Except for brief quotations in critical publications or reviews, no part of this book may be reproduced in any manner without prior written permission from the publisher. Write: Permissions, Wipf and Stock Publishers, 199 W. 8th Ave., Suite 3, Eugene, OR 97401.

Resource Publications
An Imprint of Wipf and Stock Publishers
199 W. 8th Ave., Suite 3
Eugene, OR 97401
www.wipfandstock.com

ISBN 13: 978-1-60899-647-6

Manufactured in the U.S.A.

All scripture quotations, unless otherwise indicated, are taken from the Holy Bible, The King James Study Bible, Copyright ©1983, 1988. (Previously published as the Liberty Annotated Study Bible and as The Annotated Study Bible, King James Version) Copyright © 1988 by Liberty University. Thomas Nelson Publishers.

*For my wife, Ginger,
whose encouragement, faith,
love, and objectivity contributed
significantly to Walking With Jesus*

Topical Categories in Walking with Jesus
(An Expository Commentary)

Volume One	Volume Two	Volume Three	Volume Four
The Triune God Speaks to the Saints	*Sin and Redemption*	*Christ's Prisoner*	*Walking As Mature Christians*
To the Faithful in Christ Jesus	Sin and God's Wrath	For This Cause— God's Glory	Living in Harmony With Christ
God's Will— Spiritual Blessings	God, Rich in Mercy and Grace	Revealing God's Hidden Truths	Unity in the Triune God The Holy Spirit
Trusting in Him	A Right Relationship With God	Praying to the Father	The Lord Jesus Christ
Praying for Christians	Reconciliation	Believing God's Power	God, the Father
	Praying Through the Holy Spirit		Grace According to Christ's Gifts
	God's Foundation (Apostles and Prophets)		Maturing in Christ

Volume Five	Volume Six	Volume Seven	Volume Eight
Following Christ	*Walking Wisely*	*Satan and God's Armor*	*Christ's Ambassadors*
Alienated from God	Christ-Like Conduct	Family Relationships	A Call to Discipleship
Ye Have Not So Learned Christ	No Inheritance in the Kingdom of God and Christ	Life's Basic Relationship	Wearing God's Armor
Christ-Like Conduct	Walking in the Light	The Whole Armor of God	Christ's Ambassadors
	Walking Circumspectly	Satan and His Evil Forces	
	The Marriage Relationship		
	Christ and His Church		

Ephesians "brings one into an atmosphere of unbounded spiritual affluence that creates within one's heart deepest peace and assurance. It is impossible to live habitually in Ephesians and be depressed."

Ruth Paxson

Contents

Volume Three: Topical Categories xi
Foreword xiii
Preface xv
Acknowledgments xvii
The Question of Authorship xix
Introduction xxi

1. Christ's Prisoner 1
2. Grace of God 12
3. The Effectual Working of His Power 22
4. Understanding God's Purpose 30
5. Knowing God's Plan 39
6. Bringing Us to God 49
7. God's Riches and Power 56
8. For This Cause 63
9. Strengthening Believers 72
10. The Spirit of Christ 81
11. Preparing the Heart 90
12. Love and Knowledge 99
13. Life's Foundation 110
14. Receiving Fully 118
15. Knowing the Love of Christ 127
16. The Supreme Need 134

17 Filled with God's Fullness 143

18 Being in Christ 150

19 God's Power 157

Outline Questions 165
Bibliography 205

Volume Three: Topical Categories

Category	Scripture	Chapters
For This Cause—God's Glory	Eph. 3:1	1
Revealing God's Hidden Truths	Eph 3:2–7	2–3
Knowing God's Plan	Eph 3:8–13	4–7
Praying For the Followers	Eph 3:14–17	8–13
Praying for Maturity, Understanding, and God's Fullness	Eph 3:18–19	14–18
Believing the Promises	Eph 3:20–21	19

Foreword

Robert Callahan's multi-volume work of Paul's Letter to the Ephesians is both a welcomed and long-overdue guide for Christian living today. The Apostle's sense of the eternity and greatness of God, his emphasis on the living reality and exaltation of Christ, his devotion to God's grace as an unearned gift of enduring love, and his call to an ardent and faithful discipleship all witness to an urgency and renewal critically needed in our time. Callahan's heart and style rise to meet this challenge and to convey God's message of hope and promise, of presence and courage, to Christian souls of any and every contemporary Christian tradition.

Callahan's format allows for both a devotional and studious usage. One can permit one's soul to savor every spiritual nuance the author uncovers, verse by verse, mark the passage, and return later for further nourishment. Or one can linger from text to text, gleaning with the author both theological and spiritual insight for enhancing personal discipleship, equally applicable in the arena of church and society.

The author draws on an array of insightful theological and spiritual wisdom, garnered from scholars and saints alike, theologians and missionaries. Calvin's Institutes guide Callahan's expositions, as well as the work of Markus Barth – known for his commentary on Ephesians and his delineation of Pauline theology. The author cites frequent and astute observations from Barth's exegesis of this nature. In addition, Callahan makes wise usage of Martyn Lloyd-Jones' emphasis on "experiencing the living Christ." For Lloyd-Jones, as well as the author, mere intellectual knowledge of the Christ fails to undergird one's faith or discipleship, when life's journey truly becomes sore bestead. Callahan also draws from the great 17th century theologian William Gurnall's delightful work: The Christian in Complete Armour. Perhaps students of Church history remember how both John Newton and Charles Spurgeon prized Gurnall's approach and piety and preferred it to many perspicacious studies available in their time. Gurnall's Complete Armour is known for its pithy, fervent, and wise counsel that confronts human vagaries with the truth about the self. In that respect, so too does Robert Callahan's gentle but firm counsel enrich the Christian heart and inspire one to a higher level of discipleship. No one can fail to sense this in Walking With Jesus. Whether encouraged to venture this methodology owing to his own years as a Presbyterian elder, or as an avid member and participant of the bi-annual Calvin's Colloquiums for the past 30 years, or as a fond reader of Ruth Paxson's The Wealth, Walk and Warfare of the Christian, the result is the same: a powerful, inspirational, and theologically heart-warming guide to discipleship today.

Ministers, Christian educators, seminary students, laypersons, and lovers of Jesus' life will find Callahan's work immensely valuable. His volumes deserve our grateful and sincere attention, as we too seek to walk with Jesus.

Benjamin W. Farley
Younts Professor Emeritus of Bible, Religion, and Philosophy
Erskine College, Due West, South Carolina

Preface

Paul's Epistle to the Ephesians shows us the joy and challenge of being united to Christ in his death and resurrection. It takes us from being seated with Him in the heavenlies (chapter 2), down to the battles we must wage, in His armor, with powers of evil (Eph. 6). In a balanced and judicious manner, longtime Presbyterian elder, Bob Callahan, exercises remarkable insight in opening to believers the vital truths of Ephesians; truths that once taken in, transform the attitude towards life, and often set the soul singing!

As a professor of theology, I have carefully worked through one of his multivolumed series, and found it to be theologically sound: evangelical and scholarly at the same time. It has spiritual depth and is extremely practical; it is accessible in good, clear English. It is neither a commentary, nor a series of sermons. In some ways it reminds me of some of the ancient Patristic engagements with a series of texts of Holy Scripture. It brings the reader into the presence of the Most High, and – if considered thoughtfully and prayerfully, is likely to cause him to sit down under the canopy of God's love.

The journey of Christians in today's world is very demanding indeed, and Bob's work is intended to be a guide to help every pilgrim 'Walking with Jesus.' It will be a rich resource for Sunday Schools, Bible studies, as well as for individual devotions.

Douglas F. Kelly
Reformed Theological Seminary
Charlotte, NC

Acknowledgments

The crafting of Walking With Jesus was not a "one man show" but numerous people working together to present a formidable work. Three guiding lights have been paramount in the minds of those making significant contributions: one, presenting the theology in accord with the tenets of the Reformed Faith; two, employing language that presents the Gospel in a meaningful and understandable light; and, three, expounding upon Scripture in a clear, concise, and forthright manner.

It has been God's blessing that the following ministers and theologians have enthusiastically and willingly provided their time and talents to enhance this work. They are:

- Dr. Frank Barker, Founder and Pastor Emeritus of the Briarwood Presbyterian Church, Birmingham, AL
- Dr. Benjamin W. Farley, Younts Professor Emeritus, Bible, Religion, and Philosophy, Erskine College, Due West, SC
- Dr. James C. Goodloe, IV, Executive Director, Foundation for Reformed Theology, Richmond, VA
- Dr. Todd Jones, Senior Minister, First Presbyterian Church, Nashville, TN
- Dr. Douglas Kelly, Richard Jordan, Professor of Theology, Reformed Theological Seminary, Charlotte, NC
- Dr. Norman McCrummen, Senior Pastor, Spring Hill Presbyterian Church, Mobile, AL
- Dr. Mark Mueller, Senior Pastor, First Presbyterian Church, Huntsville, AL
- Dr. Richard Ray, Former Managing Director of John Knox Press, Montreat, NC

Without the knowledge, wisdom, and encouragement of these individuals this work would neither have become a reality nor available to individuals seeking a better understanding of the teachings of the Scripture and the joy of walking daily with the Lord Jesus.

Several others have labored diligently to create this work, and to produce the finished product. Our daughter, Karen Callahan Myrick, made significant contributions during the drafting process through her knowledge of grammar. Ms. Lynn Sledge, as the copy editor, judiciously reviewed the manuscript and made valuable contributions for improving it. Four ladies, Helen Marshall, D'Anne Dendy, Kelly Comferford, and Elizabeth Annan, worked tirelessly, with dedication, to prepare draft after draft and to make positive contributions to the project. In addition, Wick Skinner's attention to detail provided valuable insight as well as enhancements to the manuscript.

It is not possible to thank them sufficiently for their dedication to making this volume a desirable repository of Christian truths, and in so doing to cheerfully work on draft after draft, to recommend enhancements, and to make appropriate changes in the text. Their unselfish contributions are too many to enumerate. May God bless them.

The Question of Authorship

Recent scholars have questioned the authorship of the letter to the Ephesians and have been less convinced that it was the Apostle Paul. However, for the sake of simplicity of expression we will abide by the traditional view and refer to Paul as its author.

Introduction

The creation of this work was the result of unusual developments which some would attribute to happenstance and others to God's providence. You may be the judge after considering the following.

During May 2000 a friend invited my wife and me to visit the Spring Hill Presbyterian Church in Mobile and hear their new minister, Norman McCrummen. We accepted his invitation.

The following March, Dr. McCrummen was preaching on anything but Ephesians when he interrupted his sermon, paused long enough to slowly scan the congregation twice, and said, "I want everyone to read the first and second chapters of Ephesians by next Sunday" and promptly returned to his sermon. The next day I called him and said, "I can't do it" a few times. Finally, his light went on and he said, "What can't you do?" I said, "I can't read the first and second chapters of Ephesians by next Sunday." He asked, "Why can't you? It will only take ten to fifteen minutes." I responded, "I have fifty-eight to sixty expository messages on the first two chapters of Ephesians that took thirty to thirty-five minutes to present." His response was, "I want to read all those and everything else you have on Ephesians." Thus began the long, arduous, and heartwarming journey of converting handwritten notes along with printed ones into the written word. It has been a joyful, though demanding experience.

Paul's Letter to the Ephesians has been described as "The holiest of the holies." My love affair with it began in the 1980's when I read a book containing great sermons of the twentieth century. The most impressive one was written by Martyn Lloyd-Jones. As a result, I read other works of his including his exposition of Ephesians. Thereafter, unexpectedly, I was asked to teach an adult Bible Study Group. They said they would provide the material, but I demurred and said, "I would gather my own material." This set in motion the process of acquiring knowledge through the best expository works available at the time on Ephesians including Martyn

Lloyd-Jones, William Gurnall, Ruth Paxson, Markus Barth, John Calvin, Otto Weber, and others.

The objective was to present the essence of Paul's letter as it was presented to him by the Lord Jesus and the Holy Spirit. Further, to mine the gold available in the fruitful works of those fertile minds that God had cultivated and enabled to expound upon the truths that His only begotten Son had revealed to His apostles and disciples. Therefore, it was a paramount obligation to express God's truths in a simple, straightforward manner according to the dictates of the Holy Spirit so that the reader may grasp it and interpret it according to the will of our Lord and Saviour Jesus Christ.

The need for the truths of the Gospel is as great today as it was in the first century. The conditions are similar and the challenges facing our culture reveal the need for knowing the living God and His Son. Today, the people of faith require the same spiritual nourishment as those brave souls of the early days after the Resurrection, who would rather face death than deny their Lord and Saviour.

There are people in responsible positions in Christ's church who deny Him by: their passivity; seeking secular acceptance; and failing to honor Him in public. These apostasies negatively impact members of organized Christian churches as well as non-believers.

They create an environment in which unrighteousness flourishes. This results in irreverence as aptly described by R.W. Dale, "Where there is irreverence for the divine law the vision of God becomes fainter; as the vision of God becomes fainter the restraints of the Divine Righteousness are lessened and at last the vision of God is lost altogether." May God enlighten us regarding His infallible Word so that we will hunger and thirst for righteousness, and for the vision of God to shine brighter and brighter as we serve Him with courage, wisdom, justice, and self-control.

This expository commentary is designed to bring individuals, whether they are spiritually children, adolescents or adults into a closer, more mature relationship with the Lord Jesus Christ. It begins with the Triune God; presents the doctrines of the Christian faith; reminds us "that we henceforth be no more children, tossed to and fro . . . but speaking the truth in love, may grow up into Him in all things, . . . even Christ." It continues by emphasizing the importance of being renewed in the spirit of your mind; putting on the new man, which after God is created in righteousness and true holiness; using the whole armor of

God to thwart the manifold attacks of Satan; and concluding with the admonition to conduct ourselves as Christ's ambassadors.

The spiritual food contained ranges from milk and honey to tough meat. The flavor of this exposition encompasses all varieties—sweet, sour, pleasant, bitter, tart, tasteless, dry, burned, and succulent. Do not reject the nourishment because of its texture or flavor, but seek to understand it despite your preferences, since it provides food for good health and strength for joyful living. May God's truths flourish in your heart and mind, and enable you to withstand the tests, trials, and tribulations that come your way as you are "Walking With Jesus."

In presenting this work, I realize everyone has different challenges. The fascinating part of God's Word is that it meets us where we are. The question is, will we meet Him there, hear what He has to say, and accept the nourishment He offers?

The words of William Gurnall are appropriate and enlightening in contemplating God's Word. He said prior to expounding upon Ephesians, "The fare that I shall be serving during the coming weeks will be from God's own table. If perchance it does not go down well or should not have the flavor that you desire, please do not despise the provider of the food, but blame the cook who has prepared it and is serving it." To that I say, Amen!

The courses being served by this cook are described herein. May they provide the taste and nourishment you are seeking.

Robert B. Callahan Sr.

1

Christ's Prisoner

For this cause I Paul, the prisoner of Jesus Christ for you Gentiles [Eph. 3:1].

The third chapter begins with an interesting statement, *For this cause I Paul, the prisoner of Jesus Christ for you Gentiles* [Eph. 3:1]. Paul was a prisoner in Rome when he wrote this. His imprisonment helped confirm his apostleship. However, there were people at that time who used this fact against Paul and his ministry. His adversaries represented his incarceration in an unfavorable light.

So, what does Paul do? He turns the tables on his opponents and detractors. He declares to the Ephesians that his chains prove his calling as an Apostle of the Lord Jesus Christ. Why? Because the only reason he was imprisoned was due to the fact that he preached the Gospel to the Gentiles. Paul's statement was a confirmation that he had discharged his responsibilities properly, faithfully, and effectively. The mind of Paul worked logically. He did not "shoot from the hip" or throw out ideas to see if they would fly or be accepted. He always had a plan with a definite purpose in mind.

When Paul says, *For this cause,* he is really saying "for this reason" or "because of this." To what is he referring? To the contents of the second chapter and the astounding truths presented in those twenty-two verses. Namely, that the Gentiles who believed the Gospel have been made one with the Jews in Christ Jesus. The thoughts presented in that chapter were,

- *You hath he quickened* (made alive), *who were dead in trespasses and sins;*

CHRIST'S PRISONER

- *But God, who is rich in mercy, . . . hath quickened* (made) *us* (alive) *together with Christ, (by grace ye are* (have been) *saved;)*
- *For by grace are ye* (have been) *saved through faith; and that not of yourselves: it is the gift of God:*
- *Not of works, lest any man should boast.*
- *Aliens from the commonwealth of Israel, and strangers from the covenants of promise,*
- *Without God in the world: But now in Christ Jesus . . . made nigh by the blood of Christ.*
- *For through him we both have access by one Spirit unto the Father.*
- *Fellow citizens with the saints, and of the household of God;*
- *Foundation of the apostles and prophets, Jesus Christ himself being the chief corner stone;*
- *A holy temple in the Lord: . . . a habitation of God through the Spirit*

[Selections from Chapter 2 of Ephesians].

Paul starts this portion of Ephesians saying he is a prisoner of Christ or, as Calvin says, an ambassador. Then almost immediately he digresses to give the Ephesians an account of his own ministry, his calling, his office, and his objective. In verse fourteen he returns to what he started to say in the first verse.

Paul stated simply and succinctly that he was not just a prisoner, but *a prisoner of Jesus Christ*. This was not idle boasting, but a dignified and faithful statement of the facts. The ignominy which was intended for Paul was transferred to the highest glory; as Calvin aptly stated, "So highly ought the name of Christ to be revered by us, that what men consider to be the highest reproach, should be to us the greatest honor." Paul commends his persecutions, saying they were endured because of the Gentiles. This must have had a positive impact on the hearers.

There is a question to consider: why did Paul interrupt his thought trend in verse one and digress from verses two through thirteen? He explains this, saying, *Wherefore I desire* (ask) *that ye faint not* (do not lose heart) *at my tribulations for you, which is your glory* [Eph. 3:13]. He urges the Ephesians and others receiving this letter not to faint, or as the Greek word *ekkakeō* is interpreted, do not "cave in" at your tribulations, but regard them as their own glory. Oh, that we would not "cave in" when facing our own tribulations. When examining this statement we realize the Apostle is concerned about others and the glory of God. These were Paul's outstanding traits.

Paul was writing to the members in Ephesus where he had resided for three years. He had not intended to write a theological masterpiece, yet this Epistle is crammed full of doctrine and theology. Paul's intention was to encourage them in the faith, establish them, increase their knowledge and faith in the Lord Jesus Christ, and present practical, logical information and reasoning.

He was expounding Old Testament teachings and Christ's earthly ministry. He was not interested in literary style or form, but in preaching and teaching the Gospel and proclaiming the spiritual life, the life *in Christ*. There were numerous times he said *in Christ* or *with Christ* in the first two chapters. Paul wanted the true believers to increase in their faith. He did not want them to stumble and fall, fade away, or "cave in."

He knew they were anxious about his state of mind, his welfare, his sufferings and tribulations. Also, he knew they would remember that he taught them previously about the blessings of the life *in Christ*; how as a child of God he was always safe; the emphasis he placed on the glorious life *in Christ*; and the fact that Christ was with him and them, and watching over His followers. Paul remembered what he had preached and taught the Ephesians. He knew all too well that the followers might suffer a serious setback if they questioned or doubted the Gospel because he was a prisoner in Rome.

At that time, as well as today and through the intervening years there has been nothing comparable to the perplexity expressed by God's people when confronted with the question of suffering. Questions are asked day in and day out: Why does God allow His own people to suffer, to endure trials and tribulations? Why should Paul, or anyone, for that matter, have to suffer? Paul addresses these questions in Philippians and in his letters to Timothy. Also, in this third chapter he digresses to deal with particular areas of discomfort, such as the pain, distaste, and suffering of the godly and righteous.

Note the approach he takes: He does not send a word or greeting expressing general or specific comfort. He does not say it is unfortunate that these things happen in this cruel world, or do not get upset because I am sure everything will be alright in the future. No, he does not do that. What does he do? He tells them how he looks at it, his own attitude and reaction. He urges them to look at the problem and to reason it out as he has done.

So questions are asked when things go awry: Why does God allow this? Why does He allow so and so to suffer? Why does He allow certain things to happen in the church as we know it today, or among the community of believers?

The Apostle makes a great statement on this whole issue and takes a positive stand. He says whatever persecution you may be suffering, whatever illness, pain, trials, or tribulations you may be enduring, or whatever disappointment you may have experienced, here is the way to face it.

First and foremost, the Apostle does not utter the first word of complaint. There is not even the slightest hint of a grumble. He does not ask whether this is fair, or state what he has done to serve God, not a word! No grumbles, no complaints.

Second, he does not hide behind a store mask and exhibit a special brand of fortitude. He does not say you have to take the good with the bad, or you have to like the rain along with the sunshine. He does not say pull your self together, be a man, show a little courage, keep a stiff upper lip. No, he does not say any of those things. Why? Because it does not have anything to do with Christ's teaching.

Third, what does the Apostle say? He is rejoicing in the midst of his trials. At times you wonder how people can spend grueling hours in preparing their minds and bodies for something and at the same time enjoy it.

Paul says in the midst of his imprisonment,

> *Wherefore I desire* (ask) *that ye faint not* (do not lose heart) *at my tribulations for you, which is your glory.*
> *For this cause I bow my knees unto the Father of our Lord Jesus Christ* [Eph. 3:13–14].

> *That he would grant you, according to the riches of his glory, to be strengthened with might by his Spirit in the inner man;*
> *That Christ may dwell in your hearts by faith; that ye, being rooted and grounded in love,*
> *May be able to comprehend* (understand) *with all saints what is the breadth* (width), *and length, and depth, and height;*
> *And to know the love of Christ, which passeth knowledge, that ye might be filled with all the fullness of God* [Eph. 3:16–19].

Paul exults in his suffering. He is triumphant, he is joyful. His vision is beyond his physical circumstances. He wants them to look beyond his present condition and theirs.

> *But I would* (want you to know) *ye should understand, brethren, that the things which happened unto me have fallen out* (turned out) *rather unto the furtherance of the gospel;*
> *So that my bonds in* (chains for) *Christ are manifest in all the palace, and in all other places;*
> *And many* (most) *of the brethren in the Lord, waxing* (are becoming) *confident by my bonds* (chains), *are much more bold to speak the word without fear* [Phil. 1:12–14].

Paul says all these things, even though they may appear to be negatives and hamper his activities, are being used by God for the furtherance of the Gospel.

Paul amplifies upon the hardships he was enduring while remaining joyful in serving the Lord Jesus. He reminds Timothy while living in harsh circumstances that *God hath not given us the spirit of fear; but of power, and of love, and of a sound mind* [2 Tim. 1:7]. Think of that comforting statement when in the midst of unfavorable conditions or trying circumstances.

He does not leave it at that. He goes on to tell us that we are not to be *ashamed of the testimony of our Lord, nor of me as his prisoner: but be thou partaker of the afflictions* (share with me in the sufferings) *of the gospel according to the power of God* [2 Tim. 1:8]. Yes, we will have afflictions of many different types, sizes, and lengths of time. However, we can focus on them or on the power of God. The choice is ours, which do you choose?

Paul informs us that when we have trying situations and difficult challenges to face that God *called us with a holy calling, . . . according to his own purpose and grace* [2 Tim. 1:9]. He tells us that although we may get down, feel sorry for ourselves, or want to give up, that it is God who has called us, who will be with us and strengthen us in our time of need.

He recognizes that Timothy is encountering difficulties in his life and ministry. He does not offer sympathy but only encouraging words and mind-strengthening thoughts. He tells Timothy,

> *Hold fast the form of sound words, which thou hast heard of me, in faith and love which is in Christ Jesus* [2 Tim. 1:13].

> *Thou therefore endure hardness* (hardship), *as a good soldier of Jesus Christ* [2 Tim. 2:3].

We are to hold fast to these words, remembering we are Christ's soldiers. We are to endure any hardship we may encounter in a joyful manner. This is the truth that Paul presents to the followers in the Way, and this doctrine is not confined to Paul. Look at Peter and what he says,

> *Beloved, think it not strange concerning the fiery trial which is to try you, as though some strange thing happened unto you:*
> *But rejoice, inasmuch* (to the extent) *as ye are partakers of Christ's sufferings; that, when his glory shall be revealed, ye may be glad also with exceeding joy.*
> *If ye be reproached* (insulted) *for the name of Christ, happy* (blessed) *are ye; for the spirit of glory and of God resteth upon you: on their part he is evil spoken of* (blasphemed), *but on your part he is glorified* [1 Pet. 4:12–14].

What a magnificent statement! This is the essence of the teaching Paul presents. He wants the Ephesians to look at his ordeal in such a way that they will see the glory of God.

This doctrine is presented by Peter and supported by other Scripture. However, an important question needs to be asked: How do we arrive at a state or condition similar to the apostles? How do we get there?

Paul did not achieve this status because of his temperament or personality. Rather, it was the end result of the approach he used. It was the result of knowing Christ, His teachings, His life, and His commands. It was knowing that he received power, strength, and might from God the Father through the Holy Ghost.

He asked questions. He noted the answers and proceeded in a logical manner. This was his method. It is something you and I have to learn. Paul did not allow things to overwhelm or depress him; he did not sit down and commiserate with himself or bemoan his fate and circumstances. We must learn to do what Paul did, put the whole matter into its proper context and relate it to our faith and life as members of the community of believers. Then certain truths will emerge.

When reading the first verse of this third chapter it should raise questions. Why was Paul a prisoner? How did he become one? What caused this to happen? What is the explanation? What is the reason?

Undoubtedly, Paul asked these and other questions. He considered the possible answers, and then the light began to dawn. Each of us needs to learn to ask questions, to seek objective answers, to look for the truth, and not to seek or adopt rationalizations.

Through this process Paul realized that he was not an ordinary prisoner. He was not Rome's prisoner or Nero's prisoner. He was not in prison because of Roman law or because he failed to do something. Then what was he doing there? He was a prisoner of Jesus Christ. Have you ever thought when things were going wrong or things were not right that what was happening to you was because of Jesus Christ, and that he was using you?

Paul states the fact directly and to the point, *I am a prisoner of Jesus Christ!* Did he say it was because of his faith, or works, or mind, or heart? No! Neither did he imply that it happened because of someone or something, nor did he imply that it was Jesus Christ. He stated it forthrightly.

One of my main peeves is with officers, teachers, and preachers who imply the wonderful name and person of our Lord Jesus Christ without ever naming Him. Paul never did that. He never merely implied anything with respect to Jesus Christ; he always named Him.

If Paul had not met Jesus Christ on the road to Damascus, he would not have been in prison, and he knew it. Had he remained the chief persecutor, he would not have been in prison.

If you are not called, and if you do not respond to Jesus Christ, then there is one thing that is true: you will not suffer in certain situations, whether they be in business, family, society, or the church. Because when you belong to Christ, when you are *in Christ*, then you must obey His commandments, and they *are not grievous*.

Paul recalled the commission that Christ gave him on the road to Damascus, when the Master said, *But rise, and stand upon thy feet: for I have appeared unto thee for this purpose, to make thee a minister and a witness both of these things which thou hast seen, and of those things in the which I will appear* (reveal) *unto thee* [Acts 26:16]. Paul was called to be a minister and a witness. We may not be called to be ministers, we may not have the gifts that Paul had, but we can be witnesses wherever God places us.

Paul wrote to the Philippians, saying, *For unto you it is given in the behalf of Christ, not only to believe on him, but also to suffer for his sake* [Phil. 1:29]. Paul tells the Philippians do not grumble or complain if you are suffering for Christ's sake, but regard it as an honor. The early

Christians realized God was working in their lives, and they thanked Him when they suffered for His sake. They recognized they were placed in situations because of their commitment to Christ. They realized that by the grace of God they could handle their predicaments and problems, and that it would be to the glory of God. Further, Paul believed his sufferings were proof of his calling and discipleship. Paul tells Timothy, *Yea, and all that will live godly in Christ Jesus shall suffer persecution* [2 Tim. 3:12].

This is a searching statement: if we live godly in Jesus Christ we shall suffer persecution in some way for it. James says, *My brethren, count it all joy when ye fall into divers* (various trials) *temptations* [Jas. 1:2]. Why? Because it is proof of your calling.

Paul says to the Colossians,

> *. . . whereof I Paul am made a minister;*
> *Who now rejoice in my sufferings for you, . . . which is behind* (lacking) *of the afflictions of Christ in my flesh for his body's sake, which is the church* [Col. 1:23–24].

"Since Paul is a member of Christ's body it is the Lord Himself who suffers when His apostle suffers. Further, these afflictions are more Christ's than Paul's. They do not detract from his ministry, but enhance it; since they exist for His body's sake, the church," as incisively described in *The King James Study Bible*.

And, to the Philippians he says, *That I may know him and the power of his resurrection, and the fellowship of his sufferings* [Phil. 3:10]. Paul believes and states that he has the great and high privilege of following in Christ's footsteps.

Peter also points this out when he says,

> *For even hereunto were ye called: because Christ also suffered for us, leaving us an example, that ye should follow his steps:*
> *WHO DID NO SIN, NEITHER WAS GUILE (DECEIT) FOUND IN HIS MOUTH:*
> *Who, when he was reviled, reviled not again* (in return); *when he suffered, he threatened not; but committed himself to him that judgeth righteously* [1 Pet. 2:21–23].

It is a privilege and a duty to follow in Christ's steps.

Finally, Paul suggests it was loyalty to his calling that led to his imprisonment. Probably a better translation of the latter part of this first verse is *the prisoner of Jesus Christ for you Gentiles*.

What does this mean? Everywhere Paul went he preached the Gospel to the Gentiles as well as to the Jews. He said the Gospel of Jesus Christ was for them as well as for the Jews. This infuriated the Jews.

The twenty-first and twenty-second chapters of Acts make it clear that the primary reason for his arrest and imprisonment was his ministry to the Gentiles. He persisted in preaching that the Gentiles were *fellow heirs* with the Jewish believers. If Paul had not emphasized this doctrine, then the Jews might have allowed him to continue preaching. Paul's teaching was intolerable, impossible to the Jews. So they opposed him and nearly killed him.

The Apostle says to the Ephesian Gentiles that he is in prison because he persisted in saying that the Gentiles could become the children of Abraham the same way as the Jews had, by faith. If Paul had not preached that truth then probably he would have been a free man. However, Paul rejoices because they have the Gospel of Jesus Christ.

That remarkable Christian, Ruth Paxson, states clearly and forcefully why Paul rejoiced that the Ephesians, and we their descendents, in the faith, had the Gospel of Jesus Christ. He wanted them to remember, remember what it was like to be without the Lord Jesus. Paxson states it with these memorable words, "'*Remember*' that apart from the blood of Christ you could never have been 'made nigh' unto God. '*Remember*' that as a Gentile, you have nothing in yourself or in your race of which to boast. . . . '*Remember*' that God has no favourites in His family, and that both Jew and Gentile have the same access unto the Father, through the Son, by the Spirit. '*Remember*' that when once either Jew or Gentile has been incorporated into Christ through faith in His blood, he is a fellow-member of Christ's Body and a fellow-citizen with all saints. '*Remember*' that 'we twain' are made, 'one new man' in Christ, . . . ye Gentiles '*Remember*' that your two most precious possessions, your Saviour and your Bible came to you through *the Jew*; that the door to the Church was opened to you by Peter, *the Jew;* and that the revelation given of your equal possession of all its blessed privileges came to you through Paul, *the Jew*. . . . and '*remember*' the Word of God spoken centuries ago to the father of the Jews." These words are as true today as they were 2000 years ago.

Paul was quite a man! He was a true follower of Christ's. In studying this portion of Scripture, '*Remember*' that our two most precious possessions, our Saviour and God's truth are revealed to us: Paul would have been more popular if he had not proclaimed certain truths. However, Paul's personal objective was not to be popular. He wanted to preach the whole truth. He did not want to ignore part of it and only present the popular or pleasant doctrines. His approach and belief was that he was commissioned to preach the whole doctrine of Christ, not just part of it.

Why is he in prison? Because he is absolutely certain that Christ died for the Gentile as well as for the Jew. Though he knew it meant prison and probably death, nevertheless he was going to preach the full Gospel. As Bob Ferguson would oft times say, "nothing more, nothing less, nothing else."

Paul's position, as well as his attitude and statements, had a significant, strengthening impact on the community of believers at Ephesus. It should have the same impact upon us, today.

Knowing Paul, the Ephesians must have said it is true. Paul is absolutely certain of it. He knows for sure that we are made one Body with the Jews in Christ Jesus. Paul's words and actions strengthened the faith of the Ephesian believers. You may feel unworthy, but when you hear or read about what others have done as they faced adversity it gives you the strength to do that which otherwise you might not do.

Paul tells the Ephesians that if they truly understand the meaning of his imprisonment, if they view it correctly, then it will bring them further knowledge of the glorious life *in Christ*. He says, in effect, the life *in Christ* is everything. It is glorious, wonderful, and more precious than his personal liberty.

Paul explains being *in Christ* more fully to the Philippians, saying,

> *For to me to live is Christ, and to die is gain* [Phil. 1:21].
> *For I am in a strait (hard-pressed) betwixt two (between the two) (life and death), having a desire to depart, and to be with Christ; which is far better:*
> *Nevertheless to abide in the flesh is more needful for you* [Phil. 1:23–24].

Paul knows he is *in Christ*. He knows that he will be with Christ through eternity, but he also knows he has a responsibility to serve Christ in the flesh. He is torn between the two. He knows that if he departs he will be with Christ and that "death is a graduation to something better: It is a promotion to the heavenly presence of Christ and perfect fellowship with Him," (King James Study Bible).

However, Paul realizes he is to do the will of God. Therefore, he says,

> ... *I know that I shall abide and continue with you all for your furtherance* (progress) *and joy of faith;*
> *That your rejoicing may be more abundant in Jesus Christ for me by my coming to you again* [Phil. 1:25–26].

Paul was intent upon serving Christ, and that was what he did regardless of the conditions he faced.

In conclusion, consider a few questions:

- Do you rejoice in tribulation?
- Are you discouraged by what has happened to you?
- Are you disappointed or dissatisfied by what is happening in the church?
- Do you suffer because of Christian doctrine and biblical truths?

Look at these things, ask questions, examine the facts, then proceed to thanking God, and giving the glory to Him, and having the ability to say with Paul, *For unto you it is given in the behalf of Christ, not only to believe on him, but also to suffer for his sake* [Phil. 1:29]. This should provide a better understanding of, *I Paul, the prisoner of Christ Jesus for you Gentiles.*

Amen!

2

Grace of God

> *If ye have heard of the dispensation* (stewardship) *of the grace of God which is given me to you-ward:*
> *How that by revelation he made known unto me the mystery* (hidden truth); *(as I wrote afore* (before) *in few words,*
> *Whereby, when ye read, ye may understand my knowledge in the mystery of Christ)*
> *Which in other ages was not made known unto the sons of men, as it is now revealed unto his holy apostles and prophets by the Spirit;*
> *That the Gentiles should be fellow heirs, and of the same body, and partakers of his promise in Christ by the gospel:*
> *Whereof I was made* (became) *a minister, according to the gift of the grace of God given unto me by the effectual* (effective) *working of his power* [Eph. 3:2–7].

Paul begins the third chapter and immediately digresses from his initial thought to the material provided in verses two through thirteen. Verses one and fourteen begin with the words For this cause. Then from verse fourteen through the end of the chapter he returns to his original intention.

During this brief digression Paul wants the Ephesians to have a better understanding of why he is a prisoner in Rome, the real reason for it, and to illuminate certain truths. A review of the first two chapters reveals Paul used the personal pronouns *I* or *me* a total of three times.

> *Wherefore I also, after I heard of your faith in the Lord Jesus, . . .*
> *. . . making mention of you in my prayers* [Eph. 1:15–16].

However, in this digression in the third chapter he uses the singular personal pronoun a total of nine times from verses two through thirteen. Why does he use the personal pronoun? To glorify God. Paul starts his digression with the phrase, *If ye have heard*, which in reality means "assuming that you know." Although he takes it for granted that they know, he proceeds to remind them. Repetition is the essence of good teaching.

Why does Paul digress at this point? For the Ephesians and us to realize what God has done for them through the Lord Jesus Christ, focus on God, have an appreciation of how He works, and how He turns very difficult situations into events glorifying His name. He wants the Ephesians to praise God as they begin to comprehend His ineffable capabilities and to have some measure of understanding regarding God's great plan and the purpose of salvation. This knowledge should comfort them and strengthen their faith.

Paul wants to give the Ephesian Gentiles a relatively quick picture of how the Gospel came to them and remind them that as pagans they were living a godless life, worshipping images and idols, and living with low moral values.

Now, they are saints in God's community along with the converted Jews, and they are worshipping Jesus Christ. That is quite an astounding development, almost incredible. The real question is, how did it happen?

When considering this question and Paul's explanation some may ask: What does this have to do with today and the current world problems? Or, what does it have to do with my family, my friends, my church, my community, and me? The answer is that the Apostle deals with principles fundamental to the Christian faith, to being *in Christ*.

Paul presents these principles because he realizes if we are not familiar with them that we could fall into grievous error. He is instructing the followers *in the way* in certain truths. He says, *ye have heard of the dispensation* (stewardship) *of the grace of God which is given me to you-ward*. He is describing what was given to him by God and why. Then in the following five verses he points out several things, saying,

> *How that by revelation he made known unto me the mystery* (hidden truth);
> *Whereby, . . . ye may understand my knowledge in the mystery of Christ)*
> *Which in other ages was not made known . . . as it is now revealed unto his holy apostles and prophets by the Spirit;*
> *That the Gentiles should be fellow heirs, and . . . partakers of his promise in Christ by the gospel:*

> *Whereof I was made* (became) *a minister, according to the gift of the grace of God, . . . by the effectual* (effective) *working of his power* [Eph. 3:3–7].

Paul says he has been entrusted with this stewardship by the grace of God.

Once again, in Paul, we see the extraordinary provision God has made for our salvation. He reiterates God's purpose of uniting the Gentiles and Jews, and that his message has been revealed through the *holy apostles and prophets by the Spirit.* Paul is still amazed by the fact he has been called to be an Apostle, and he continues to be astonished by the grace of God. He says this grace has been *given me.* The office to which he has been called is the result of God's grace. This includes the idea that God equipped him to be an Apostle and bestowed upon him certain gifts.

Paul points out that he had been given the Gospel of salvation so that others may understand it. He amplifies upon this idea and supports it saying, *Let a man so account of* (consider) *us, as of the ministers* (servants) *of Christ, and stewards of the mysteries* (hidden truths) *of God* [1 Cor. 4:1]. God takes certain men and makes them stewards and custodians of the message of His redeeming grace.

When thinking about this, go back to the first chapter of the Acts of the Apostles. The apostles Jesus had chosen were assembled together in Jerusalem and had been told to remain there to *wait for the promise of the Father, . . .* (and) *ye shall be baptized with the Holy Ghost not many days hence* [Acts 1:4–5]. While the apostles were waiting, they asked Jesus,

> *. . . wilt thou at this time restore again the kingdom of Israel?*
> *And, he said unto them, . . .*
> *. . . Ye shall receive power, after that* (when) *the Holy Ghost is come upon you: and ye shall be witnesses unto me both in Jerusalem, and in all Judea, and in Samaria, and unto the uttermost part of the earth* [Acts 1:6–8].

Remember, the apostles had been with Jesus during His earthly ministry. They knew the facts about His life, death, and resurrection, but they were not in a condition where they could preach and witness effectively. They could not do that until they had received the fullness and the power of the baptism of the Holy Spirit. When they received it, they could go out, and they did.

Paul says that the stewardship of this amazing mystery of God's grace has been given to him, that God has filled him with His Spirit, and enabled him to understand it, so he could preach, teach, and perform miracles among the Jews and Gentiles.

Paul talks about being *stewards of the mysteries* (hidden truths) *of God* [1 Cor. 4:1]. What is meant by the term *mystery* or *mysteries*? It occurs only in the New Testament and primarily in Paul's Epistles. Normally, when we think of it, we conjure up ideas of novels, or plays, or television programs, or unsolved crimes. Then, when we know who perpetrated the act, it is no longer a mystery. In the New Testament sense, a *mystery* is a secret which has been or is being disclosed; but, and this is important, since it is a divine secret it remains a mystery and does not become transparent to most people.

Please note, Jesus said *Unto you it is given to know the mystery* (hidden truths) *of the kingdom of God: but unto them that are without* (on the outside), *all these things are done in parables* [Mark 4:11]. This is the only time in the four Gospels that the word *mystery* is used. Jesus is saying the kingdom of God is a mystery, because it is the kingdom of God, and its knowledge is given only to those to whom it is revealed, just like the knowledge of Christ.

Paul uses this word properly to reveal the secrets of God. The essence of the revelation is the mystery of the Gospel, as stated by Paul in his letters to the Ephesians and to the Colossians,

> *And for me, that utterance may be given unto me, that I may open my mouth boldly, to make known the mystery* (hidden truth) *of the gospel* [Eph. 6:19].

> *That their hearts might be comforted* (encouraged), *being knit together in love, and* (attaining to) *unto all riches of the full assurance of understanding, to the acknowledgment* (knowledge) *of the mystery of God, and* (both) *of the Father, and of Christ* [Col. 2:2].

Paul informs the Ephesians of the truth that the Gentiles as well as the Jews are included in God's divine purpose regarding salvation. To Paul this is a mystery not because its inestimable wealth actually overwhelms him, but it overturns his mindset based upon previous experiences and learning. It is also especially true of the Jews.

The Greeks were familiar with the term *mystery*. Especially since it was used to describe the secret rites into which the worshippers were initiated in the so-called mystery religions. Paul uses this term in order to convey to the Greeks, and others familiar with it, the Gospel of Christ.

Paul says the mystery has been revealed to him. It is not something vague and indefinite, but plain and clear. The truth itself is clear, but because of its character it cannot be attained or achieved by the natural man or mere human ability. This is because man is finite and sinful. Therefore, he cannot understand it through his own limited capabilities. He needs divine revelation. Probably, the classic statement on this particular truth is the following:

> *But as it is written,* EYE HATH NOT SEEN, NOR EAR HEARD, NEITHER HAVE ENTERED INTO THE HEART OF MAN, THE THINGS WHICH GOD HATH PREPARED FOR THEM THAT LOVE HIM.
> *But God hath revealed them unto us by his Spirit: for the Spirit searcheth all things, yea, the deep things of God* [1 Cor. 2:9–10].

The mystery was that the Gentiles were to enter into the fellowship of promise and become partakers in the life of Christ through the Gospel. The calling of the Gentiles was the mystery of Christ, and it was achieved under the reign of Christ.

Paul emphasizes that the mystery and the knowledge of it was revealed to him. It was not knowledge that he acquired on his own or through his own ability. He had received the revelation directly from our Lord Jesus Christ. He also had a dispensation, or a better modern word is commission, to preach and teach. He had a divine command.

Why does Paul state that the mystery had not been known, when the prophets of the Old Testament foretold so many things? The prophets had declared that people shall come from all over the world to worship God. Further, that the worship of the true God would spread abroad throughout the whole world, and Christ's kingdom would stretch from the east to the west and all nations would be subject to Him. The apostles quoted from the later prophets and from Moses. This raises the question: How could something which had been proclaimed by so many actually have been hidden? Why does Paul say that without exception they have been in ignorance?

Paul's words must not be understood in the context that there had been no knowledge on those subjects. "The prophets prophesied out of the certainty of revelation," as affirmed by Calvin, but they left the manner and the time undetermined. They knew that God would communicate His grace to the Gentiles, but they did not know when, or how, or by what means. It may seem remarkable that there was this type of ignorance among the apostles. However, they had heard it from the prophets, but undoubtedly remembered that the Master said, *other sheep I have, which are not of this fold* (flock), *them also I must bring, and they shall hear my voice; and there shall be one fold, and one shepherd* [John 10:16]. However, the apostles did not understand this statement at the time.

There were other verses which the apostles did not fully comprehend:

> *. . . Go ye into all the world, and preach the gospel to every creature* [Mark 16:15].

> *. . . ye shall be witnesses unto me both in Jerusalem, . . . and in Samaria, and unto the uttermost part of the earth* [Acts 1:8].

"The apostles initially recoiled from calling the Gentiles," according to John Calvin. They did not know how this was to be accomplished. Actually, before the event occurred there was confusion about Christ's words. It can be said there was a type of veil over their eyes. Therefore, it is perfectly appropriate for Paul to call it a mystery and say that it had been hidden, until it was revealed.

Hopefully, we are seeing something of the Christian truths. It is not ordinary knowledge. It is not something that the human intellect by itself can comprehend. The Gospel truths remain hidden to the natural man and to the princes of this world when the Holy Spirit does not provide the necessary enlightenment. Paul stresses this point when he says, *Now we have received, not the spirit of the world, but the spirit which is of God; that we might know the things that are freely given to us of God* [1 Cor. 2:12].

This is not an ordinary truth that the Apostle Paul is describing. He is saying whatever the power of our minds may be, no matter how brilliant we may be, it is not enough. We need the Holy Spirit present and working within us before we can begin to receive and understand God's divine truth. This is hard for some to accept. We are dependent solely and exclusively upon Scripture. There is no saving truth apart from what we find in God's Holy Word.

Paul uses the term *mystery* twice in the six verses we have been considering. The first time he uses the word he is referring to the general mystery, or the mystery of Christ. The second time he is concerned about a particular mystery, a mystery that is now revealed unto his holy apostles and prophets by the Spirit. This mystery is that the Gentiles shall be *fellow heirs*. Note the statement, *That the Gentiles should be fellow heirs, and of the same body, and partakers of his promise in Christ by the gospel* [Eph. 3:6].

This refers to the relationship of the Jew and Gentile in the community of believers. Paul glories in the fact that he is an "apostle to the Gentiles." He did this so the Ephesian Gentiles and pagans who had become followers in the Way would realize the marvel and wonder of their salvation.

"That the Gentiles were to be saved and that they were to be blessed through the promise given to Abraham was revealed in the Old Testament. But that God purposed to create this new man out of Jew and Gentile, and constitute them one Body over which Christ would be the Head, and in which the Gentile would be co-equal with the Jew in every respect, was indeed a new thing. Jews and Gentiles are to be fellow-partakers in everything in Christ," as proclaimed by Ruth Paxson. Paul's words to the Ephesians were powerful and had a definite impact on both the Jews and Gentiles.

When considering this particular mystery it is well to examine other points and obtain a better understanding of Scripture. First, it is not the primary objective of preaching and teaching to exhort and comfort people. The basic objective is to instruct the hearers, because only as one grasps the doctrines of faith in Christ can a person truly live and enjoy life as one is meant to do.

What is the answer to this teaching? *And the scripture, foreseeing that God would justify the heathen* (Gentiles) *through faith, preached before the gospel unto Abraham, saying, IN THEE SHALL ALL NATIONS BE BLESSED* [Gal. 3:8]. And our Lord said to Peter, *upon this* (large) *rock I will build my church* [Matt. 16:18]. Peter preaching at Pentecost said,

> . . . *Repent, and be baptized . . . in the name of Jesus Christ for the remission* (forgiveness) *of sins, and ye shall receive the gift of the Holy Ghost.*
>
> *For the promise is unto you, and to your children, and to all that are afar off* [Acts 2:38–39].

This is obviously a reference to the Gentiles.

We have considered the two mysteries: the mystery of Christ and the mystery of God's purpose being manifest and functional. The community of believers is the form it takes until it is completed.

What does this mean? That all are together *in Christ* sharing God's blessings through the Holy Spirit. We are fellow heirs, fellow members of His Body, and fellow partakers of the promise *in Christ* revealed by the Gospel. This is by God's grace.

Amen!

3

The Effectual Working of His Power

Whereof I was made (became) a minister, according to the gift of the grace of God given unto me by the effectual (effective) working of his power.
Unto me, who am less than the least of all saints, is this grace given, that I should preach among the Gentiles the unsearchable riches of Christ [Eph. 3:7–8].

When proceeding to the seventh and eighth verses of the third chapter, we become aware of certain truths the Apostle was identifying for the Ephesians. They are:

. . . I was made (became) a minister, according to the gift of the grace of God given unto me by the effectual (effective) working of his power.
Unto me, . . . is this grace given, that I should preach among the Gentiles, the unsearchable riches of Christ [Eph. 3:7–8].

The Apostle Paul wanted each and every member of the community of believers in Ephesus to know that they were fellow heirs with Jesus. Why was this true? Because of the Gospel and the effectual working of God's power. The Apostle expresses his own amazement that he was called to be a minister of the Gospel of the Lord Jesus Christ. Note what he says, *Unto me, who am less than the least of all saints, is this grace* (of God) *given.*

This statement is not to be considered modesty, affectation, or hypocrisy. Paul never ceased to be amazed by the fact that he who had been the chief persecutor, who had been blasphemous, and had been injurious to the development of *the way* was called to proclaim Christ's Gospel. Further, he had been given the privilege of being the Apostle to the Gentiles.

There is a doctrinal truth worth repeating at this point: The essence of the new teaching is that we should very definitely realize it is by grace that we are saved. And we are what we are by the grace of God.

Paul realized that he was what he was by the grace of God. He knew his deficiencies and shortcomings, yet he was still amazed at what God had done for and through him. Though Paul labored long and hard, traveled many miles, and encountered difficulties and opposition, ever present in his mind was how little he had done, how much more he might have done, and how much God through Christ had done. These amazing facts led him to explain how it happened, saying,

> *Whereof I was made* (became) *a minister, according to the gift of the grace of God given unto me by the effectual* (effective) *working of his power.*
> *Unto me, who am less than the least of all saints, is this grace given, that I should preach among the Gentiles the unsearchable riches of Christ* [Eph. 3:7–8].

Note, Paul says *the gift, given, the grace of God, by the effectual* (effective) *working, of his power*. He realizes everything had been given through grace by God's love, mercy, and compassion. Note Paul also says *by the effectual working*, which means by the energetic working of His power, and by the in-working of His power. He uses this word to explain what turned a persecuting, blaspheming hater of Christ into an Apostle for Christ.

This raises a vital question. What causes a person who persecutes, blasphemes, and ignores God into one who loves, obeys, and serves Him? The Apostle says there is only one answer: *The effectual working* of God's power through His grace. Paul had been changed, he had been born again, and he had been regenerated. He had become a new creation. How had this taken place? *By the effectual working of his* (God's) *power*.

It was *the effectual working* of this power that changed his life. He was called to the ministry. Others of us are called to other means and methods of serving our Lord. Remember, it is *the effectual working of his power* that makes us followers. It is not something you and I do; it is done to us and for us. All is given by God. Paul says, *Whereunto I also labor, striving according to his working, which worketh in me mightily* [Col. 1:29].

Paul states in Colossians that he is striving in his labors, but it is the result of what God is doing to him and in him. It is God *which worketh mightily in me.* Here we see the wonderful blending of the divine and the human. We see the power of God energizing a person and enabling him to carry on His work.

Paul in writing to the Colossians "... does not speak, however, only of the outcome of his preaching (though in that to the blessing of God appears), but also of the efficacy of the Spirit, in which God manifestly showed Himself. For he rightly ascribes his superhuman efforts to the power of God, which, he declares, is seen working powerfully in this matter," as Calvin states with humility based upon revealed knowledge, thanks to "the efficacy of the Spirit."

Paul says in these two verses that he *was made* (became) *a minister* and *should preach among the Gentiles the unsearchable riches of Christ*. What a remarkable, profound, and sublime statement! Each Christian is called to share *the unsearchable riches of Christ*. This applies to preachers, teachers, and evangels. Therefore, when we look at both the negative and positive aspects of this statement, what do we find?

We are not to spend our time teaching and preaching about current events. People wonder about in-depth expositions of Scripture, when what they hear on television and read in the papers or periodicals focuses attention upon political, economic, and international situations. Some feel that teaching and preaching should address subjects such as these; however, they are not the areas of our expertise.

It is not the responsibility of the teacher or minister to preach patriotism. The world was in turmoil when Paul wrote to the Ephesian followers. And if you think about it, the world has been in turmoil ever since, and this year is no exception.

Neither is it proper to simply teach or preach a moral code or urge a general moral ethic upon the hearers. The world can preach morality and ethics. The philosophers have done so. The Jews in the first century AD taught morality. But Paul says the call is to preach *the unsearchable riches of Christ*.

This may cause some consternation. It is not our business to merely preach religion or godliness in a general manner, tell people to pray at certain times and in certain ways, or conform to certain standards and adopt suggested disciplines. Islam does all that very effectively. Remember, Paul had been a Pharisee and he did these things, but that is not what he means by preaching *the unsearchable riches of Christ*.

Further, it is not our primary business to adopt certain portions of Scripture to support a point of view on a worldly or local issue.

What then does Paul preach and teach? Primarily and essentially the Lord Jesus Christ Himself. What are the riches? *The unsearchable riches of Christ.*

The essence of the Gospel is what Christ gives to us and what we receive from Him. This thrills Paul and motivates him. Therefore, Paul states the first thing that happened to him as a minister was a gift from God, a gift of God's grace.

What is to be preached and taught? First, the Gospel is Christ Himself: He is *the unsearchable riches*, He is the message of Christianity and its Gospel, everything is in Him and nothing is apart from Him. To have anything, we must have contact with Him and be in Him. We are united to Him, and we are to draw from Him. Though what He gives is of vast importance, it takes second place to what and who He is.

Second, the word *unsearchable* in Greek means "not traced out." The riches are untraceable, unsearchable, in that a person cannot get at them on his own. It requires effectual power. It requires the Holy Spirit.

Third, the riches are such that no one person can ever fully and completely comprehend them. As Paul continued his ministry, he was more and more amazed at these riches.

Fourth, the riches can never be fully described, because they are beyond our finite capabilities. These riches are glorious and endless in their availability and blessings.

Fifth, they are inexhaustible; they will never fail. They can never decrease, grow dim, or diminish. Of course, a question is: what are these *unsearchable riches of Christ*? Look at what Paul says to the Corinthians, *But of him are ye in Christ Jesus, who of God is made unto* (became for) *us wisdom, and righteousness, and sanctification, and redemption* [1 Cor. 1:30].

The Apostle says the first thing needed is wisdom, then knowledge and understanding. Why do we need wisdom? The world as we know it, or as we live in our environment, confronts us with many questions when considering problems, possibilities, and perplexities. Therefore, there are questions to consider. What is it all about? Why is man as he is? Is there a God? Why isn't God doing something about different situations? Why is there suffering? Why isn't there some stability?

Wisdom in the face of these questions and our daily situations is needed. But the question is, what type of wisdom? How can we achieve this wisdom? The Apostle says, it is in Christ, *who of God is made unto* (became for) *us wisdom*. By this he means we obtain absolute perfection of wisdom *in Christ*. "The Father has revealed himself fully in Him. This is true in order that we may not want to know anything apart from Him," as John Calvin sheds additional light on this matter.

The Lord Jesus Christ teaches us about our Father. He makes us conscious of our sinfulness, but He also makes us aware of the righteousness available in Him. When you believe on the Lord Jesus Christ your sins are forgiven, and you are clothed with His righteousness. Therefore, you can go into the presence of the Father, due to Christ's righteousness, not yours. He atoned for your sins by His death and shed blood. His obedience is imputed to us for righteousness. This righteousness is part of *the unsearchable riches of Christ*. But there is more.

We are still confronted by the lusts of the flesh and the mind. We still have temptations, and we will continue to do battle with the evil one. The natural man is still present. So what does Paul say? He says Christ *is made unto* (became for) *us wisdom, and righteousness, and sanctification, and redemption.*

Christ is our sanctification. He helps us mightily in our daily lives by providing the Holy Spirit within us and the ability to grow in the Lord. Because of Him, we shall one day stand faultless and blameless before God.

Paul means that we, who are unholy by nature, are born again by His spirit into holiness, so that we may serve God. From this we gather, as Calvin says, "that we cannot be justified freely by faith alone, if we do not at the same time live in holiness. For those two gifts of grace are inseparable, they are tied together by a firm tight bond, and if anyone tries to separate them or pull them apart, then he is in a sense trying to tear Christ to pieces."

Anyone desiring holiness of life must realize it comes only through a life *in Christ*, and by the power of the Holy Spirit. You cannot be saved by faith without at the same time laying hold of Christ for holiness of life. Our faith opens the door to the heart, but it is our Saviour and the Holy Spirit who do the work of sanctification.

This may come as a jolt to some. Certainly there has been a heavy emphasis upon justification and free righteousness by faith. However, this passage clearly shows that faith lays hold of regeneration, just as much as the forgiveness of sins. These two gifts, righteousness of faith and sanctification, are intertwined, yet distinguishable.

The Apostle also tells us that Christ is our redemption. What does this mean? He has purchased our pardon by dying on the Cross. He has atoned for our sins. He has done for us what we could never do for ourselves. Redemption is the first gift of Christ to be started in us, and it is also the last one to be brought to completion.

Paul in this passage from 1 Corinthians identifies the benefits *in Christ*. He does not say that Christ has been given to us as something to be added to or built upon with respect to our wisdom, righteousness, sanctification, and redemption. But, the Apostle does say that he *who of God is made unto* (became for) *us wisdom, and righteousness, and sanctification, and redemption*. Totally, fully, and completely! We do not contribute or make up one particle of one percent. It is all of God and nothing of ourselves.

This passage of Scripture gives us a clear description of the offices of Christ. It should also, as Calvin expressed it, "give us the best understanding of the force and nature of faith." When Christ is the proper object of our faith, we should then know what benefits He gives to us.

Christ Jesus *is made unto us wisdom, and righteousness, and sanctification, and redemption*. Note it says, *is made unto* (became for) *us*. Not any of it is made by us individually.

Do you see why it is important to consider the details, the phrases, the thoughts, the context, and the individual words?

- *In the beginning was the Word. The Word* is Christ. It is through *the Word*, through Christ, that God reveals Himself to us and that we have life.

- What does Christ say? *I am come that they might have life, and have it more abundantly* [John 10:10].

- Life means life in the Spirit, in fellowship with Christ, and in a positive relationship to God.

- It does not mean participating in the pleasures of the world, or in seeking diversions that will enable one to forget certain things temporarily.

Jesus says, *he that cometh to me shall never hunger; and he that believeth on me shall never thirst* [John 6:35]. Jesus is the One that provides true life. He possesses the riches and gladly imparts them. Yet it is as I know Him and possess Him that I am a participator in His riches. Why does anyone ever think that he or she should receive the riches without participating? This fact is often overlooked or ignored.

The Apostle has personal knowledge of the Lord Jesus Christ. That is his greatest treasure. Therefore he shares it with us that we might embrace it.

A commitment to Christ means we are to know Him. He will reveal Himself, but we must open our minds, hearts, eyes, ears, and books. Further, we must pray for understanding, knowledge, and faithfulness, just as Paul did and says.

Paul lived in a state of communion with Christ. Christ was nearer, dearer, and more real to him than anything in the world. All the treasures and riches of God are *in Christ*. He will come into a person's heart, into one's life, and He will dwell there.

What are some of the riches we receive by being *in Christ*?

- The gift of the Holy Spirit. John the Baptist told us that when Christ would come He would *baptize you with the Holy Ghost* [Matt. 3:11], that we receive by His power.
- He gives us rest. Jesus said, *Come unto me, all ye that labor and are heavy laden, and I will give you rest* [Matt. 11:28].
- Peace is given unto us. Jesus said, *Peace I leave with you, my peace I give unto you* [John 14:27].
- Joy. Jesus said, *ask, and ye shall receive, that your joy may be full* [John 16:24].
- Wisdom and knowledge. *In whom are hid all the treasures of wisdom and knowledge* [Col. 2:3].
- Contentment. *I have learned in whatsoever state I am, therewith to be content* [Phil. 4:11].
- An inheritance. *To an inheritance incorruptible, and undefiled, and that fadeth not away, reserved in heaven for you* [1 Pet. 1:4].

These are some of *the unsearchable riches of Christ*. This strength and power is available to us when we get down, discouraged, depressed, or are concentrating on ourselves. Then we need to turn to Christ and let Him come in. Remember, He stands at the door and knocks. This is a message for the converted, and the unconverted.

Jesus spoke plainly and forthrightly to the members of the Church at Laodicea. He tells them their works were neither hot nor cold. He cautions them, saying, *knowest not that thou art wretched, and miserable, and poor, and blind, and naked.* He counsels them to *buy of me gold tried* (refined) *in the fire,* so that they would have certain things. He rebukes and chastens them, and tells them to *be zealous therefore, and repent.* Yet, He is available and *will come in to him, and will sup* (dine) *with him, and he with me.* He encourages them, saying, *To him that overcometh will I grant to sit with me in* (on) *my throne,* He foretells that He will be *set down with my Father in* (on) *his throne* and, He forewarns them, saying, *He that hath an ear, let him hear what the Spirit saith unto the churches* [Selections from Rev. 3:16–22].

The unsearchable riches of Christ are available to us. We are not to be like the members at Laodicea. We are to show forth the sanctification working within us.

We are called to be holy. We are to be obedient. We are to know Him and know that He will abide with us. Thanks be to God for the words of Jesus and His love.

Amen!

4

Understanding God's Purpose

> *And to make all men see what is the fellowship of the mystery, which from the beginning of the world hath been hid in God, who created all things by Jesus Christ:*
> *To the intent that now unto the principalities and powers in heavenly places might be known by the church the manifold (many-sided) wisdom of God,*
> *According to the eternal purpose which he purposed in Christ Jesus our Lord* [Eph. 3:9–11].

When considering the Gospel of Jesus Christ, the unsearchable riches, the mystery, salvation, and eternal life, we normally think of these things in the personal vein. However, God's message in the Gospel goes beyond the personal to something greater and larger.

It is important to recognize and deal with the key points of self and one's mindset. These two items habitually get in the way of our relationship to God, understanding God's purpose, and having communion and fellowship with the Lord Jesus Christ. Consequently, we need to understand what the Apostle is saying, in detail.

When doing so, we need to consider often-asked questions. What does the Bible say about the world situation? What does the church say? What is Christ, or Christianity, doing about the problems confronting mankind? Is there any hope? Why does God not bring peace? Why is there suffering?

These are realistic, legitimate questions that should be addressed. Therefore, we need to examine and understand what the Apostle is say-

Understanding God's Purpose

ing in these three verses. Remember, what Paul says was given to him by our Lord Jesus. It is not his personal opinion.

The first thing to note is that there is darkness when the Apostle says that all men should see. The verse was translated from the Greek as follows: *to make all men see what is the fellowship of the mystery*. However, the Greek word for *see* in this verse is *phōtizō*. Actually, it means "to enlighten," and this is the only time it is used in the Bible.

Therefore, the verse should read "to enlighten all men (as to) what is the fellowship of the mystery." The Apostle declares this in order for the fellow partakers to understand what is going on with respect to world events, life, history, and man. There are many theories put forward, but Christ wants us to know what is going on according to God's plan and His purpose.

There are many expectations about what is happening in the world. "Arnold Toynbee, the renowned historian, said that the whole process of history, in a sense, is a matter of cycles," as stated by Martyn Lloyd-Jones. There is a rise, then a fall. There are ups and downs. A nation comes to power and stimulates others; then decay and decline set in, and the powers fall. Then the process repeats itself.

Of course, other individuals and groups have their theories—the philosophers, sociologists, humanists, hedonists, and so on. But the question is: what does the Bible say? God has a plan and a purpose for the world, which the Bible reveals. The theme of this "book of books" is to give men an understanding of life in this world and why things happen.

The followers *in Christ* should have a unique understanding of the world and what is happening. If we don't, then there is something wrong with us. We are to have an understanding of God's plan if we are to overcome the darkness and to be enlightened. We have this responsibility as Christians, or followers *in the way*.

Second, the Apostle says that God had hidden His plan from the ages until Christ came and began to reveal it with the words *which from the beginning of the world hath been hid in God*. Paul evades the prejudice of novelty. He declares that it had been hidden in God. This statement is contrary to the thinking of many people who cannot accept the idea that they should be ignorant of anything, or that God has the right to conceal His purposes until He chooses to reveal them.

This strikes at the heart of the matter, that God is wiser than we are. That is why Paul calls them *the unsearchable riches of Christ*. By this he means that although they exceed our ability to grasp them, they deserve our reverence and admiration. Therefore, our rashness, lack of forethought, and impetuousness must be suppressed when God's divine foreknowledge is revealed.

When considering these truths it is not only important but necessary to remember that God is not subject to the flux of time. He looks down on time and the world. He is above it all. There is nothing contingent about God's plan. He does not have to improvise, modify, or change it because of what someone else may do or has done.

Third, the Apostle says that this truth has been hidden by using the words *the fellowship of the mystery*. This means that even though it had been previously hidden, it is now the will of God that men share in His purpose.

This brings up a crucial question. What is this plan, which God had purposed before the foundation of the world, which had been hidden from men and angels, which is in being, and is in the process of being carried out? That is quite a question!

The Apostle reminds us that it is God's world. He refers to creation, but the context in which he presents it refers to redemption and regeneration along with their blessings to us. Yes, God created the world. He brought light from darkness. He brought the world into being. He made it perfect. However, it is not what it was meant to be because of sin.

Therefore, God sent His only begotten Son. It is by Him and through Him that the Gentiles are restored to the whole. It is through Him that light comes out of darkness, as Paul noted in his Second Letter to the Corinthians: *For God, who commanded the light to shine out of darkness, hath shined in our hearts, to give the light of the knowledge of the glory of God in the face of Jesus Christ* [2 Cor. 4:6]. From the creation of the world Paul declares that it is God who enlightens the darkness. How is God going to accomplish His purpose in Jesus Christ?

Man has succumbed to sin. Consequently, sinful conditions exist in the world. God's plan is to redeem and to restore it. He is going to reunite everything through Christ, since He has purposed to restore all things *in Christ*.

As stated previously, it is not going to be achieved by simply preaching the ethical teachings of Christ. It is not a matter of ethics or a moral code. That is a fatuous and foolish supposition. Further, it is a denial of Christ's ministry and Gospel.

If the only thing necessary was for men to follow Christ's teaching and example then the law given through Moses would have been the answer. However, the children of Israel, the people of God, failed completely. No one kept the law. No, not one.

The law was perfect, but man could not keep it, and that is the difficulty. Man is not capable of keeping the law. If a person cannot keep the Ten Commandments, then how can he or she possibly live by the Sermon on the Mount?

The Apostle, in this third chapter, endeavors to magnify to the followers in Ephesus the mercy of God to the Gentiles, and the immense value of the Gospel. He declares that in preaching the Gospel the *manifold wisdom of God* is made known. The wisdom of God was made manifest by uniting the Jews and Gentiles in the fellowship of salvation.

Again, we must caution ourselves to consider the whole as well as the individual parts and not concentrate on just one particular idea. For example, the Jews thought that the wisdom of God was confined to dispensation under the law.

However, God brought forth another instance of His wisdom by making the Gospel available to all men. It was not a new wisdom, but it was more complete than our limited capacity to grasp it. We need to remember that the knowledge we have acquired, that has been revealed to us, is only a slight portion of the total. We need to keep in mind the purposes for which God appointed the ministry of His Word. Preaching serves the need of men among whom it is used. It reveals the wonderful wisdom of God, which was not known previously.

They see new truths, which before being revealed were hid in God. It is by God revealing His Word that people progress. How does God accomplish His purpose in Christ Jesus?

It is not that Christ tells us what we have to do. Please note and remember that it is not by saying what you are to do, or by establishing a list of "do's" and "don'ts." God's great purpose is brought about by what Christ has done for us. It is not by what you and I do. Remember, we are the clay, He is the Potter. What God has done and is doing through Christ results in His divine purpose being achieved. Therefore, the question is: What do we need to do in order to realize His divine purpose?

We need to be reconciled to God. We need to be in a right relationship with Him. We will not be blessed while we are His enemies or estranged from Him. This is achieved through Christ. The enmity and estrangement must be removed. It is accomplished through the Lord Jesus, who adopts us and makes us His children.

God has placed our sins upon Christ. He has punished the sinful acts and the condition of sin in Christ. Therefore, God looks at us and forgives us when we sincerely seek forgiveness. How do we realize a right relationship to God?

Paul provides a beautiful description of what is involved with respect to each of us coming into a right relationship with God. First, *And all things are of God* [2 Cor. 5:18]. The Apostle means all things belong to Christ's kingdom. If we wish to be Christ's, we must be regenerated by God. Regeneration is not an ordinary gift. Paul is speaking of the grace of regeneration, which God confers upon His elect. This gift is bestowed not as the Creator and Maker of heaven and earth, but as the Creator of His Church by refashioning His people into His own image. The believers are admonished to live for God.

Second, *who hath reconciled us to himself by Jesus Christ* [2 Cor. 5:18]. There are two main points: man's reconciliation with God, and the means by which we obtain it. The whole Gospel is directed to these two points.

Under the first point, God hath reconciled us to Himself by Christ, and under the second, He did it by not reckoning unto men their trespasses. This grace is given by Christ through the Gospel, so we can share in it.

Third, there has been *given to us the ministry of reconciliation* [2 Cor. 5:18]. This is a remarkable description of the Gospel's mandate: We are to be messengers of God's good will, to comfort the godly, and to assure them that God is dealing with them and wants them to return to His grace. This is the main purpose of the Gospel.

Ministers have the duty and authority to preach the good news and to assure us of God's fatherly love. The minister is God's ambassador. Therefore, he has an awesome responsibility. Woe to the scribes and Pharisees and their present day counterparts.

Fourth, *God was in Christ, reconciling the world unto himself* [2 Cor. 5:19]. The Apostle says *God was in Christ*, and by His intervention He was reconciling the world to Himself. Further, he says that the Father is in the Son.

Jesus said, *If I do not the works of my Father, believe me not. But if I do, though ye believe not me, believe the works: that ye may know, and believe, that the Father is in me, and I in him* [John 10:37–38]. Whereas God had been distant, now He has drawn near in Christ. Why has God appeared to men in Christ? For reconciliation, to end the hostility, and for them to become heirs, *joint-heirs* with Christ.

Fifth, *not imputing their trespasses unto them* [2 Cor. 5:19]. How do people return to God's favor? By being regarded as righteous, and by obtaining remission of their sins. Paul informs the Ephesians of a beautiful fact, saying, *According as he hath chosen us in him before the foundation of the world, that we should be holy and without blame before him in love* [Eph. 1:4]. We were loved before the foundation of the world.

Scripture explicitly teaches that God the Father's wrath has been placated by the Son's sacrifice, and God had mercy upon people; therefore, the Son was offered for the expiation of men's sins. Why? Because God had mercy upon them, not because of any merit on their part.

Wherever there is sin there is also God's wrath, for God is not favorably disposed toward us until our sins are blotted out by not imputing them to us. We cannot grasp this truth apart from Christ's sacrifice and shed blood. Therefore, Paul is right to make it the basis of our reconciliation.

Sixth, *God was in Christ, reconciling the world unto himself, . . . and hath committed unto us the word of reconciliation* [2 Cor. 5:19]. The Apostle says again that a commission has been given to the ministers of the Gospel to bring the message of reconciliation to the members of the community of believers. Paul reaffirms that the message has been given to him and to the other apostles. It is the responsibility of the ministers and teachers to spread the fruit of Christ's suffering, death, and resurrection.

There are those who say that this message is applied in some magical or mysterious manner and that only a very few have the ability to perform this magic. This was true of the Papists prior to and during the Reformation concerning the salvation of souls.

The reconciliation or restoring us into a right relationship with God is not performed by marble statues, or fictitious and frivolous superstitions. The only way ministers or teachers or anyone can restore us to

God's favor in a proper and orderly manner is by bearing witness to us through the Gospel and advising us that we can be reconciled to God by His grace through Christ. Then, the Holy Spirit will work within us.

Testimonies regarding the truths contained in the Gospel are to be presented again, again, and again to the believers. Anything else is just an imitation or counterfeit. Our confidence is to be in the Gospel, the Gospel alone, and God's grace. "Ministers of the church are ambassadors for testifying and proclaiming the blessing of reconciliation only on the condition that they speak from the Gospel as providing a legitimate warrant for what they say," as John Calvin explicitly stated the condition for proclaiming the Gospel to the sheep in their respective pastures.

Seventh, *as though God did beseech you by us* [2 Cor. 5:20]. God did "call you to one's side" (His side) by His apostles and by His ministers. The vital question of eternal salvation depends upon the testimony of God. It is far too important to depend upon the assurances of men. We are to be sure that God has appointed the ministers and that He speaks to us through them. We are to be knowledgeable of Scripture regarding Christ's teachings. Why? So that we cannot be led astray!

Eighth, *we pray* (implore) *you in Christ's stead* (behalf) [2 Cor. 5:20]. Scripture says *How beautiful . . . are the feet of him that bringeth good tidings* (preach the Gospel) [Isa. 52:7].

What we need for our complete blessedness, and without which we are most miserable, is bestowed upon us only through the Gospel. There is no other way. It is the responsibility of the ministers and teachers to open the Gospel, to present it, and to allow the Word of God to work within us.

Ninth, *be ye reconciled to God* [2 Cor. 5:20]. There is one thing to bear in mind always and never lose sight of: Paul is writing to believers, to followers in the Way. Yet he feels compelled to state these truths repeatedly. Should we do any less?

The work of the apostles, ministers, and teachers is perpetual forgiveness, so that we are perpetually in God's favor. The Gospel promises the forgiveness of sins through our Lord Jesus Christ. We know that we receive forgiveness through Christ by the one great sacrifice He made. And, we know that we receive forgiveness by the free unmerited grace of God.

Tenth, *For he hath made him to be sin for us, who knew no sin* [2 Cor. 5:21]. Sin is opposed to righteousness. Paul teaches explicitly that we were made righteous as a direct result of Christ having been made sin and assuming our sin. That is the only way.

When talking of righteousness in this respect, we are describing something imputed, or attributed, to us. It is not one of our qualities, habits, or capabilities. It is the righteousness of Christ.

Eleventh, *that we might be made the righteousness of God in him* [2 Cor. 5:21]. The first thing to note is that the righteousness of God does not mean the righteousness that God gives us, but rather it means the righteousness of God that makes us acceptable to Him. Paul illuminates upon this, telling the Romans, *For all have sinned, and come* (fall) *short of the glory of God* [Rom. 3:23]. This means that we have nothing in ourselves by which to glory before God. We may receive the praise of men, but the praise of God is more important. The Apostle John reminds us of the attitude of many when he says, *For they loved the praise of men more than the praise of God* [John 12:43].

How can we become righteousness before God? In the same way Christ became a sinner. He took our sins upon Himself and became the offender in our name, and was reckoned a sinner because of us. Therefore, in the same way we are righteous in Him. Because we are judged according to Christ's righteousness, which we have put on by faith. Scripture says, *For he hath made him to be sin for us, . . . that we might be made the righteousness of God in Him* (Christ).

What is required when God looks at us and forgives us? A new creation. This is a vital part of the Gospel. Man in sin is in such a condition that nothing can deal with it except a new creation.

What does God do in Christ? He brings into being a new creation, a new body, a new humanity, and a new man *in Christ* containing both the Jew and Gentile. All the old divisions are abolished, and a new being is created. This is an ongoing process. God gathers them together and prepares them. This is part of God's grand purpose and design. Further, it will be carried on until it is completed. When it is completed, Christ will return as King of kings and Lord of lords. And when it is accomplished, all sin, iniquity, and evil will be eliminated.

Since this will happen we should focus attention on what the Bible says regarding regeneration. Jesus said to Peter and the other disciples, *Verily I say unto you, That ye which have followed me, in the regeneration when the Son of man shall sit in the throne of his glory, ye also shall sit upon twelve thrones, judging the twelve tribes of Israel* [Matt. 19:28]. This is an enlightening statement by the Master. It reveals our days in eternity with Christ will continue forever and ever.

Some things which the world regards as being of vital importance are not even mentioned in the Bible, such as world leaders and the powerful nations of the twentieth or twenty-first centuries. The Bible does not deal with trivialities, or with the rise and fall of nations. It reveals that God's plan moves steadily forward towards its completion and fulfillment. His plan will not be modified by human beings or special interest groups. We must be prepared for a few surprises as the plan unfolds.

We may think that everything is going wrong. Churches may be empty or nearly so, and people may ask, what about God's plan? What is God doing? Of course, the answer is that the churches have experienced a paucity of members or attendees at various times in the past, but then God sends a revival. If it is His will, He will send another revival or He will withhold it.

There are several points to emphasize and remember. God's plan is always in the terms of Jesus Christ, everything is fulfilled in Christ, and all God's blessings come through Him. These blessings are bestowed upon those in the real church, the community of believers, and the true Christian, the person *in Christ*, may expect to receive them, but not those who are outside Christ. As long as there is sin, lust, and passion, there will be fighting and wars, and no lasting or true peace until Christ returns, but when He does, peace shall reign forever and ever.

What is your reaction to this particular message? Are you disappointed, depressed? Were you looking for something else? These questions generate certain things to ponder: A Christian, or follower in the Way, is not just interested in personal comfort and solace; the person *in Christ* is concerned about the glory of God and the completeness of His Holy name; relevant preaching and teaching provide great help in our daily lives; and God's truth explains why the world is as it is and describes God's purpose and plan, which are being carried out.

Those who reject the Gospel because it does not give them temporary comfort, or those who reject the Lord will find themselves rejected. They will not be in the company of the Lord, nor will they reign with Christ.

We need to thank God for the light of the Gospel. It shows the world as it is, and that God is still on His throne. Further, "His purpose and plan are being carried out by those who are truly members of Christ's body," as stated by Martyn Lloyd-Jones.

Amen!

5

Knowing God's Plan

> *To the intent that now unto the principalities and powers in heavenly places might be known by the church the manifold* (many-sided) *wisdom of God* [Eph. 3:10].

The Holy Spirit revealed to the Apostle Paul much about God's plan and the person of our Lord Jesus Christ. Paul was specifically trained, prepared, and educated for the task to which the Lord Jesus Christ personally called him. He had a magnificent mind. He had a special insight into the desires, questions, needs, problems, temptations, and, yes, the shortcomings of the community of believers. In addition, he received one tremendous and glorious benefit: the Holy Spirit revealed the truths of God and Jesus Christ to him.

But Paul did not boast about this wonderful blessing. He humbled himself and turned to God in prayer. He studied and searched the teachings of the Old Testament. He talked with the other apostles, researched items, and took great care to present the teachings of Christ and the doctrines of God to the followers *in the way*.

He knew their backgrounds, their capabilities, their limitations, their education or lack of it, and then he composed his letters. He did it with forethought and with the blessing of the Holy Spirit. Paul informs the Ephesians that he *was made* (became) *a minister . . .* [Eph. 3:7]. *To the intent that now unto the principalities and powers in heavenly places might be known by the church the manifold* (many-sided) *wisdom of God* [Eph. 3:10]. That statement often times may be glossed over or read rapidly, then almost as rapidly forgotten. However, it is important to consider Paul's words and the truths contained in them.

- To whom are these truths given? ... *unto the principalities and power.*
- Where? ... *in heavenly places.*
- That what might happen? That it *might be known by the church.*
- That what might be known? ... *the manifold* (many-sided) *wisdom of God* [Eph. 3:10].

Paul labors to show God's mercy toward the Gentiles and the value of the Gospel to the Ephesians. He states forcefully that *the manifold* (many-sided) *wisdom of God* is declared in the preaching of the Gospel, and that it had not previously been made known even to the angels in heaven. The wisdom of God was manifested by uniting the Jews and Gentiles in the fellowship of salvation, and this revelation should be the most wonderful news to the men and women of Ephesus.

Unfortunately, man is accustomed to selecting the parts he wants to consider, and rejecting the items he does not want to accept or recognize. He loves to rationalize. He will ignore both the whole and individual aspects which do not suit his fancy. For example, the Jews thought that the wisdom of God was confined to the law, but God made available the Gospel to the Gentiles and others, thereby revealing another instance of His wisdom.

This new revelation was more complete and comprehensive than what He had revealed theretofore. If the calling of the Gentiles is revered by the angels in heaven, then it certainly should be glorified by people on earth.

When considering these truths we should "Keep in view the purposes for which God appointed the ministry of His word," as John Calvin adroitly observed. Note he says, "appointed the ministry of His word." "Appointed" in this sense implies providing complete and elaborate information, nothing less.

Therefore, the preaching and teaching of the Word among men is to be complete and full. The preaching and teaching of the Word serves the needs of the people. The community of believers is a mirror in which the angels contemplate the magnificent wisdom of God, which they had not known previously. The angels saw new works that had been hidden in God, and it is in this way that they progress. Should we not do the same?

What is there about *the manifold* (many-sided) *wisdom of God* that Paul is trying to reveal? What understanding does he wish to impart? There are several thoughts to consider, when examining the wonderful truths Paul presents in the remainder of this third chapter and in the balance of this magnificent Epistle.

"First, salvation in and through Christ is the ultimate and greatest manifestation of God's wisdom. We will define this wisdom as the attribute by which God arranges His purposes and plans, and the means for achieving them. I believe we can agree that wisdom is a rare faculty and quality that enables a person to view a situation properly and allows one to decide what to do and how to do it," to quote and paraphrase Martyn Lloyd-Jones.

Remember, there is a difference between wisdom and knowledge. Wisdom is the capacity and ability to use knowledge. A person may be knowledgeable, but if he or she lacks wisdom then his or her accomplishments will be greatly diminished. A significant truth revealed by the Bible is that wisdom is one of God's inherent characteristics. The Apostle tells us that this attribute is revealed *unto the principalities and powers in heavenly places* in greater measure than ever before.

When studying Scripture, we have a tendency to want to move on, to get to the next chapter, book, or letter, and to cover much material. Consequently, we may overlook an important truth or fail to grasp it.

What about God's wisdom? Have you ever noticed how He turns complexity into simplicity? We admire this capability in an artist, teacher, musician, or athlete. They make it seem simple. Should we not admire the simplicity of God's handiwork? The pattern of a flower, the ebb and flow of a tide, the consistency of the seasons, and the stars in the sky.

Certainly, we should consider the history of man and the developments that occurred after God called Abram. How does the simplicity of history, the people involved, and God's wisdom fit together? Consider the history of the Israelites, a pagan people. Abram was called, he left his own country, and entered a strange land. God formed a nation, and created a people for Himself, including Ishmael, Isaac, Esau, Jacob, and others. God used sinners, and intervened with Joseph going into Egypt, with Pharaoh and the plagues. God was present in crossing the Red Sea, in the wilderness, going into the promised land, in captivity, in establishing the kings, and in calling the prophets.

Through all this history, we see the wisdom of God. When it is revealed, we catch glimpses of God's wisdom in the variations, tints, colors, and hues, as well as the breadth and depth of them. If it does not do anything else, it should lead us to declare and proclaim: how great thou art!

Second, it is through the medium of the community of believers that God's wisdom becomes manifest. Think of a very bright white light and that light shining into a prism. What do you see? You see all the colors of the spectrum. You see an amazing variety, but also the transcendent glory of it.

When looking at the church in a biblical sense, you see it as the assembly of God in Christ. The *ecclesia* is "the process, the coming together." The term in and of itself means nothing more than an assembly. It becomes something much more and much different when God is at the center. *Ecclesia* is to be understood in the terms of its event character, actually occurring and taking place. The complete gathering of the assembly, the coming together of a fortuitous number of people.

In the Old Testament it is not one specific gathering, but the coming together of the people predetermined by Yahweh, by God. In the New Testament, *ecclesia* is the coming together. It is simultaneously the "community" (the subject of what is always actually coming together) and the "church" (as the enduring reality, which is represented and realized concretely in each individual gathering.)

The varying translations of *ecclesia* as "assembly," "community," and "church" are not to be considered in competition with one another. In reality, each one belongs to the other. Every assembly is the community and simultaneously the church. But no one assembly is the church, for everyone is dependent upon every other one.

Paul describes in a simple yet beautiful way how the church, the community of believers is to function. He makes an analogy between the body and the community of believers, which each and every one of us should understand. He says,

> *For the body is not one member, but many.*
> *But now hath God set the members every one of them in the body, as it hath pleased him.*
> *But now are they many members, yet but one body.*
> *And the eye cannot say unto the hand, I have no need of thee: . . .*

> *Nay, much more those members of the body, which seem to be more feeble (weak), are necessary:*
>
> *For our comely (presentable) parts have no need: but God hath tempered (composed) the body together, having given more abundant honor to that part which lacked:*
>
> *That there should be no schism (division) in the body; but that the members should have the same care for one another.*
>
> *And whether (if) one member suffer, all the members suffer with it; or one member be honored, all the members rejoice with it.*
>
> *Now ye are the body of Christ, and members in particular (individually).*
>
> *And God hath set some (appointed these) in the church, first apostles, secondarily prophets, thirdly teachers, after that miracles, then gifts of healings, helps, governments, diversities (varieties) of tongues*
>
> [Selections from 1 Cor. 12:14–28].

This description should enable us to better understand the importance of each member, to more fully respect the different offices of the church, and to more deeply appreciate with thanksgiving, upon thanksgiving, the inexhaustible abundance of gifts received from God.

The roots of this particular church doctrine are found in the "quite casual and unselfconscious designation of the Christian community in its local embodiments as the church of God," as understood and expressed by Alan Richardson. It is the church of God in Christ.

The church is the Messianic community. It is not an assembly of individuals who of their own free will and volition decided to get together. Rather, it originates in the redemptive act of God in Christ and continuously lives through its unity with Christ in His death and resurrection by the indwelling of the Holy Spirit. This should help us understand the doctrine of the Body of Christ, and the church being the bride of Christ. Is it any wonder that "The Christian church is more wonderful than anything seen in nature," as Martyn Lloyd-Jones exclaimed?

Third, God manifests His wisdom in salvation. Remember, Paul says to the saints in Ephesus *now unto the principalities and powers in heavenly places might be known . . . the manifold* (many-sided) *wisdom of God.* When God manifests His wisdom in salvation, what do we see?

We see the amazing way in which He handles the problem of sin. Certainly, this was not an easy problem. The most difficult problem is man in sin! Therefore, God's great wisdom was needed to solve this problem. Probably, it is His most remarkable feat of wisdom.

People who think differently do not really know the Old Testament or the New Testament. People say God is love, and since He is, then do not worry; He will forgive you of your sins, do not worry about them! That is not what Scripture reveals. The problem of salvation, even the salvation of a single soul, the forgiveness of sins, and a right relationship with God is the most profound problem there ever has been. It is the root cause of all other problems, whether they be with husband and wife, family, church, local community, state, and national or international affairs. God needed to devise an infallible plan, and He had to carry it out.

The essence of the problem is that God is not only love, but He is also just, righteous, and holy. To further complicate the problem, He cannot deny Himself. He had to develop a plan to satisfy all the characteristics of His being.

Therefore, if God is to forgive sin He must do so in a way that not only manifests His love, but also His justice, righteousness, holiness, truth, glory, and unchangeableness. Further, how does He reconcile His mercy with His righteousness? Each one of these magnificent attributes had to be perfectly maintained.

God found a way. He found a way to fulfill the law and to forgive the sinner. He reconciled His own love, justice, mercy, and righteousness. Nothing but the eternal wisdom of God could have done this. It was in this way, and in this way only, that God could remain unchangeable and perfect.

Certainly, we detract from His glory if we think of forgiveness and salvation as being easy and simple. Only God could solve the problem. To do so He had to send His own Son into the world to live among men; live under the law and obey it perfectly; assume the sins of all, go to the Cross, shed His blood, and die; and be buried, rise again, and be seen by His followers. It was in this way that God remained just, righteous, and merciful.

It is appropriate to consider the great truths conveyed to Timothy by Paul, *And without controversy great is the mystery* (hidden truth) *of godliness: God was manifest in the flesh, justified in the Spirit, seen of angels, preached unto the Gentiles, believed on in the world, received up into glory* [1 Tim. 3:16].

The renowned theologian, John Calvin, offers additional light and understanding to Paul's statement to Timothy with these enlightening words: *"Great is the mystery of godliness* . . . to prevent God's truth from being esteemed at less than its true worth because of human ingratitude, he declares its true value by saying that the secret of godliness is great, because, . . . it does not deal with common themes but with the revelation of God's Son, in whom are hidden all the treasures of wisdom.

"The most fitting description of God's person is contained in the words 'God *manifested in the flesh.*' First, we have here a distinct affirmation of both natures, for he declares Him to be at once true God and true man. Secondly, he takes note of the distinction between the two natures, for he first calls Him God and then declares His manifestation in the flesh. And, thirdly, he asserts the unity of His Person by declaring that it was one and the same Person who was God and who was manifest in the flesh.

"*Justified in the spirit.*" As the Son of God emptied Himself by taking upon Him our flesh, so also there appeared in Him a spiritual power that testified that He was God. This passage has been interpreted in different ways but I am satisfied with explaining the apostle's meaning as I understand it and shall add no more. First, justification here means an acknowledgement of divine power, as in Ps. 19.9 where it is said that God's judgments are justified, that is, wonderfully and completely perfect. . . . Thus what we read here means the same as if Paul had said that He who appeared clad in human flesh was at the same time declared to be the Son of God, so that the weakness of the flesh in no way detracted from His glory.

"By the word 'Spirit' he includes everything in Christ that was divine and superior to man, and this he does for two reasons. First, since Christ had been humbled in the flesh, Paul now contrasts the Spirit with the flesh by making clear His glory. Secondly, the glory worthy of God's only begotten Son, which John teaches us was seen in Christ [John 1:14] did not consist of outward show or earthly grandeur but was almost completely spiritual.

"*Believed on in the world.* It was above all things wonderful that God should have given an equal share in His revelation to profane Gentiles and to the angels who were the everlasting inheritance of His Kingdom. But this great efficacy of the preached Gospel whereby Christ overcame all obstacles and brought into the obedience of faith those who seemed quite incapable of being subdued—this was no ordinary miracle. So completely closed and shut was every way of approach that nothing appeared to be less probable. And yet by an almost incredible victory, faith conquered."

Christ brought the Jew and the Gentile together. He made each one see their respective conditions and then made of them a new creation. According to the flesh they may still be a Jew or a Gentile, but they have become new creations *in Christ*. That is the wisdom of God.

God also controlled events not only in Judea but also throughout the world. Several developments reveal God controlling events until the timing was right, or unto the fullness of time. The children of Israel had had sufficient time to see and realize that the mere possession of the law could not save them. At the same time, God gave the Greeks sufficient time to see that their philosophers and philosophy could not save the world, and could not resolve the problem of sin. And the political prowess of Rome impacted upon the people, but could not solve man's primary problem. However, the Roman Empire facilitated the spreading of the Gospel. When Paul was led to reveal these truths he employed a vivid intellectual interest in the Gospel of the Lord Jesus Christ. To Paul it was a revelation of the most wonderful and surprising truths concerning God and His relationship to mankind. These revelations stimulated and stretched his intellectual powers to strenuous activities, and to discerning God's will.

To Paul, the Gospel was always fresh, always new, always revealing, and always a blessing. He believed the kingdom of God was continually being revealed to him and that it was always moving forward.

Some scholars believe that whenever there have been great religious movements and reform it has been accompanied by intellectual interest in revealing God's truths in Christ, and that certain forgotten germane aspects of the Gospel have been recovered.

Certain theological definitions have been challenged, some discredited, but the actual facts themselves have been examined. Some of the central principles of the Gospel have received new applications concerning an individual's conduct and the structure of his social life.

However, in all those ways there is normally a fresh and renewed interest in the truths of the Gospel. Many times this leads to a keener awareness of Jesus Christ and a more earnest relationship with Him.

"If religious truth does not meet the just demands of the intellect as well as of the moral nature, it will be regarded with languid interest and will at last be either silently abandoned or rejected with open hostility and scorn," as asserted and described by R.W. Dale.

Paul also employed a heart and an imagination filled with infinite and eternal blessings as noted in *which is the earnest* (down payment) *of our inheritance until the redemption of the purchased possession, unto the praise of his glory* [Eph. 1:14].

Paul, believing in *the unsearchable riches of Christ*, knew that for human weakness, there is divine redemption; for human sin, there is divine forgiveness; for human uncertainty and doubt, there is divine illumination; for human fears and needs, there is free access to God; and for human limitations and restless discontent, there is ineffable strength, righteousness, and mercy in our union with the Lord Jesus Christ.

How can we rediscover and recover both the confidence and enthusiasm of Paul? Not by dwelling on the external, incidental, and superficial benefits of accepting the Gospel of Christ. It comes through an intimate knowledge of the Lord Jesus Christ, and receiving the divine truths of God.

Throughout history there have been people who have defended the Christian faith. A biographer of Voltaire speaks of the defenders of the Christian faith as having been reduced to "the humiliating necessity" of relying upon political expediency. They should never have to do so, because in stooping to such a position they surrendered their whole case.

This leads to considering certain false suppositions that are widely held and espoused:

- stating that where the authority of God is recognized that the difficulties realized by human governments are lessened,
- apologizing for trying to persuade men of the infinite love revealed in the life and death of Jesus Christ,
- pleading that we give consolation and patience to the poor because their miseries are brought about by the institution of property and the hard-heartedness of the state,
- arguing that by preaching the judgment to come we are strengthening the desire to accept common virtues which contribute to the peace and welfare of nations, and
- urging the nonbelievers to accept and practice certain teachings of Christ because they will be good for them and will bring peace.

These tenets, though well-intentioned, miss the essence of Paul's teaching as it was revealed to him.

Paul's faith expressed itself in revealing the great truths of God, in presenting the Lord Jesus Christ, and in making Him known to the followers. It was expressed by assuring them of the real tenderness, yet at the same time the unsurpassable strength, of God's love and His manifold wisdom in providing for our salvation. This was Paul's faith. It was part and parcel of his invincible energy and contagious enthusiasm.

Pray God that it may be part and parcel of our faith.

Amen!

6

Bringing Us to God

According to the eternal purpose which he purposed in Christ Jesus our Lord:
In whom we have boldness and access with confidence by the faith of (in) him.
Wherefore I desire (ask) *that ye faint not* (do not lose heart) *at my tribulations for you, which is your glory* [Eph. 3:11–13].

Once again it is important to consider a verse which often may be overlooked. This particular truth is part of the sentence beginning at verse eight and continuing through the twelfth verse. Paul provides a wealth of information for our elucidation and instruction. What do these verses reveal? *The unsearchable riches of Christ; The fellowship of the mystery . . . hid in God; Unto the principalities and powers in heavenly places might be known;* and *the manifold* (many-sided) *wisdom of God.* And to these statements now add and ponder *In whom we have boldness and access with confidence by the faith of* (in) *him.*

Paul was writing to the Ephesian followers urging them to keep from being distressed or upset regarding the trials and tribulations they were enduring. The Apostle wants the followers in the Way to understand and accept the fact that the ultimate purpose of Christ's doctrines and teachings is salvation itself and being in a right relationship with God.

We need to be reminded of these truths because it has become commonplace to think of salvation and its benefits in different terms from what was originally intended, especially in terms of particular blessings or satisfying personal needs. The primary objectives of salvation are to bring us into God's presence, worship Him, to pray to God the Father earnestly, and to have fellowship with the Lord Jesus.

There is a tendency to focus one's attention on the words *boldness and access with confidence* and to ignore or overlook *by the faith of (in) him* (Christ). It is by faith in Christ that we obtain boldness and access. It is not the other way around.

The eminent John Calvin provides additional insight into Paul's words saying, "... here we have [a] remarkable and most valuable teaching, for Paul expresses elegantly the power and nature of faith, and the confidence necessary for the true invocation of God.

"First Paul calls it 'the faith of Christ', meaning that faith ought to contemplate what is exhibited to us in Christ. Hence it follows that a bare and confused knowledge about Christ must not be taken for faith, but that which is directed to Christ, in order to seek God in Him; and this can only be done when the power and office of Christ are understood. He says that first confidence and then, as its result, boldness, are begotten of faith. Thus there are three steps to be taken. First we believe the promises of God; next, by resting in them, we conceive confidence, so that we may have a good and quiet mind. From this follows boldness, which enables us to banish fear, and to entrust ourselves courageously and steadfastly to God.

"A trembling, hesitating, doubting conscience will always be sure proof of unbelief, but a firm, steady conscience, victorious against the gates of hell, will be sure proof of faith. To trust in Christ as Mediator, and to rest with assurance in God's fatherly love, to dare boldly to promise ourselves eternal life, and not to tremble at death or hell, this is, as they say, a holy presumption."

Paul wants the Ephesians (and us) to know that this faith in Christ is available. They are not to feel sad, or perplexed, or to dwell on developments other than the ongoing presence of God. When they focus on God, their trials, tests, and troubles will take on a new perspective. As a result they will praise God and glorify His name.

This sounds nice and simple, like the thing to do, but it is difficult because *self* gets in the way. Therefore, the Apostle says, *Wherefore I desire* (ask) *that ye faint not* (do not lose heart) *at my tribulations for you, which is your glory.*

He is telling them not to faint, not to be troubled, and not to be unhappy over their situation. He is joyful because he is in contact with the eternal God and has access to Him. Therefore, Paul presents certain truths he wants us to know, digest, and put into practice. Why? Because doctrine is designed to provide a practical result for Christ's followers.

This is important. God's truth is not solely for the purpose of stimulating the mind or the intellect. It is not an end in itself, nor is it meant to be something you can discuss and argue about and then leave alone. No! Doctrine is available and designed for one purpose: to bring us to God. It is meant to be practical and applicable.

The twelfth verse of this third chapter is an excellent illustration of this principle. The Apostle introduces a profound truth, yet he wants to move us to positive action and into a closer relationship with God through our Lord Jesus Christ.

Paul's feet were planted firmly on the ground. He was not theoretical, nor did he just want to discuss various terms or ideas. He wanted practical results. Doctrine and theology are never isolated in Scripture. They always lead to application.

Paul's letters present doctrine, but it always leads to the practical application. We see an illustration of this in the third chapter. The first eleven verses lead us to the twelfth and thirteenth ones. Paul did this by design.

The application is most important. We cannot know the fullness and joy of our life *in Christ* unless we know and understand doctrine. The two go together. Doctrine must not be separated from the practical, or the practical from the doctrine.

One of the problems confronting members of different churches is that they are too consumed with doctrine, while others are not interested in it. We need to maintain a balance between doctrine and application in our daily lives.

Paul has been reminding the Ephesian Gentiles that they had been aliens and strangers; were without hope; were without God in the world; had been made fellow heirs with the saints; were fellow members with the Jews; and were fellow partakers of the great promises. Further, they should rejoice in these things in their current situation because they *have boldness and access with confidence by the faith of* (in) *him*. Think of that, think of the wonderful blessings we have as members *in Christ*, that we have access to God in prayer.

Note in this twelfth verse Paul uses *we: In whom we have boldness and access*. We all have access. There is no such thing in Scripture as religious groupings where only the ministers and priests have access to

God, but not the members or laity. That teaching or idea is not scriptural. Paul says, *we have boldness and access with confidence.* That means all of us who have been called and are members of Christ's Body.

What does Paul mean when he says under the influence of the Holy Ghost, *we have boldness, access,* and *confidence?* "Boldness" means determination to do what is right according to God's plan and calling. Also, boldness does not succumb to hesitancy, doubt, or uncertainty. Nor does it act foolishly or irrationally.

Think of certain truths. God reconciles Himself to us through Jesus Christ. The effect of this particular grace is that it admits us into His presence. Paul begins verse 12 by saying, *In whom,* which means *In Christ.*

Two things should be noted upon examining this Scripture: first, it is through Christ and faith in Him that we go into the presence of God; and second, any other way or approach is excluded. Paul elegantly expresses the power and nature of faith as well as the confidence necessary in a remarkable and valuable lesson.

Calvin expresses it very well, saying that as we consider the meaning of faith we "ought to contemplate what is exhibited to us in Christ. A bare and confused knowledge about God must not be taken for faith." But true faith can be realized only "when the power and office of Christ are understood."

Possibly, this can be better illustrated by stating that, first, there is an initial confidence, then progress, and finally boldness. This occurs in the following manner: believing in God's promises; developing confidence in them; acquiring by the grace of God the proper mindset; generating boldness; and entrusting ourselves courageously and steadfastly to God, our heavenly Father. This does not happen in the twinkling of an eye or overnight. It requires different periods of time for different people for God to work in them through the Holy Spirit.

A trembling, hesitating, doubting conscience will always confirm unbelief, whereas a firm, steady, confident conscience will always confirm faith. Confidence is necessary for true invocation and is a key to opening the gate to the kingdom of heaven. James expounds upon this confidence, saying, *But let him ask in faith, nothing wavering* (not doubting). *For he that wavereth* (has doubts) *is like a wave of the sea driven with the wind and tossed* [Jas. 1:6]. *For let not that man think that he shall receive anything of the Lord* [Jas. 1:7].

Second, *access* means "a leading unto" in Greek. It helps when considering this verse to note that this little word also means "permission, liberty, ability to enter, approach, and to communicate with." It also means "entree" or "freedom of entry." It may help to think of it in terms of gaining admission to an exclusive club. You are known, and you have all the rights and privileges of membership.

Paul uses the term to demonstrate that a relationship exists between us and God whereby we know and have confidence that we are not only acceptable to Him, but looked upon with favor by Him.

There was a gentleman who had lived in New York City for many years and had applied for membership in the prestigious New York Yacht Club. Every morning he would walk by the Yacht Club and say good morning cheerfully to the doorman, but he never, ever received a response to his greeting during the time his application was being considered. Late one evening the membership committee looked favorably upon his application since there was an opening, and they accepted him as a member. The next morning he followed his customary route to his office and as he approached the New York Yacht Club the doorman beamed, smiled, and heartily said, "Good morning Mr. Jones." Why? Because now he was a member of the Yacht Club, he had access, he was looked upon with favor, and he had all the rights and privileges of membership.

This word *access* is interesting and worth considering when examining this portion of Scripture. In the oriental world, the king's court usually had an individual responsible for bringing visitors or newcomers into the royal presence. Anyone seeking an audience with the king would have to obtain the goodwill or approval of this person in order to be introduced into the royal presence.

The Apostle Luke reveals to us the importance of receiving the proper introduction and recommendation. After his conversion and three years of indoctrination under the tutelage of the Lord Jesus, Paul went to Jerusalem endeavoring to meet with the church leaders he had previously persecuted. They rejected him, as Luke vividly describes:

> *And when Saul was come to Jerusalem, he assayed* (tried) *to join himself to the disciples: but they were all afraid of him, and believed not that he was a disciple.*
> *But Barnabas took him, and brought him to the apostles, and declared unto them how he had seen the Lord in the way (on the*

> *road), and that he (Jesus) had spoken to him (Paul), and how he (Paul) had preached boldly at Damascus in the name of Jesus.*
> *And he* (Paul) *was with them coming in and going out at Jerusalem* [Acts 9:26–28].

It was Barnabas who introduced Paul to the apostles in Jerusalem and vouched for him. Paul had to be introduced by the right person, and then he had the liberty of access.

The Greek word for *access* signifies one who introduces another as an intermediary. The biblical understanding of God as King of all the earth made it possible to use this language in describing access into God's presence. The person did not possess the independent right of access, but it was secured for him by the position and/or work of another, in this instance Christ Himself.

This word *access* throws additional light on the subject and symbolizes the decisive introduction and admission of the sinner (you and me) into the presence of God and the subsequent liberty and freedom of entry that is bestowed upon us.

Scripture informs us that we have the right of access into the presence of God. Paul says to the Romans, *we have access by faith into this grace wherein we stand, and rejoice in the hope of the glory of God* [Rom. 5:2]. Paul also says to the Ephesians, *According to the eternal purpose* (of God) *which he purposed in Christ Jesus our Lord: In whom we have boldness and access with confidence by the faith of* (in) *him* [Eph. 3:11–12].

Boldness and access, as described above, change our relationship with God through Christ, since separation from God is the position of every person as a sinner. *For all have sinned, and come* (fall) *short of the glory of God* [Rom. 3:23]. Therefore, there is a desperate and necessary human need to gain entry into the presence of God, and someone is required to do that. The state of separation and the removal of all its barriers are the result of Christ shedding His blood on the Cross. This secured our right of access into the presence of God and our justification as sinners. Paul provides additional insight saying, *For Christ also hath once suffered for sins, the just for the unjust, that he might bring us to God, being put to death in the flesh, but quickened* (made alive) *by the Spirit* [1 Pet. 3:18]. This right of access is to God Himself, through the Lord Jesus Christ.

Thus, the change in the relationship between God and man is the result of the blood shed on the Cross. Paul's statement to the Ephesians,

In whom we have boldness and access with confidence by the faith of (in) *him* (Christ), emphasizes the freedom of entry which is the right of those who have true faith in the prevailing effectiveness of Christ's work. This term *access* as used by the Apostle is a strong one, and is full of meaning.

It leads to the third word *confidence*. Confidence is always at the end of the process. When a person has confidence in something it means that he or she has practiced it diligently and is confident of using it. This is true of riding a bicycle or playing a musical instrument. Throughout the New Testament we are taught that confidence is an essential element of prayer.

We are to focus our attention upon a second principle. What is it that makes freedom of entry into God's presence possible? How can we have this *boldness and access with confidence*? The answer is stated twice in this verse, *In whom* and *by the faith of him*. This is a basic, fundamental truth, and it should be obvious. Yet people often leave it out or ignore it.

Remember, Jesus said, *I am the way, the truth, and the life: no man cometh unto the Father, but by me* [John 14:6]. Paul supports Christ's revelation by saying to Timothy, *For there is one God, and one mediator between God and men, the man Christ Jesus* [1 Tim. 2:5].

A central message of the New Testament is that there is no possibility of prayer or entry into the presence of God except in and through our Lord Jesus Christ. Christ is the only way. There is no entrance into the presence of God except through Christ. If there was any other way, then Christ did not need to come into this world and shed His blood. Why do we say there is no possibility of prayer or entry into presence of God except in and through our Lord Jesus Christ?

Other questions may be asked: Why do we say this? What about the Old Testament teachings? These questions need to be examined, and they will be as we proceed to grow in our relationship with Christ with *boldness and access with confidence by the faith of* (in) *him* (Christ).

Amen!

7

God's Riches and Power

> *But ye are not in the flesh, but in the Spirit, if so be that the Spirit of God dwell in you. Now if any man have not the Spirit of Christ, he is none of his.*
>
> *And if Christ be in you, the body is dead because of sin; but the Spirit is life because of righteousness.*
>
> *But if the Spirit of him that raised up Jesus from the dead dwell in you, he that raised up Christ from the dead shall also quicken* (give life to) *your mortal bodies by* (because of) *his Spirit that dwelleth in you* [Rom. 8:9–11].

In the Old Testament God gave instructions for worship, God instructed the Israelites how to build the temple, God called Moses to the mountain, and God gave the Ten Commandments. Why were these things provided? Because God was teaching His people about holiness, as well as His majesty, and His eternity.

He taught them there was only one way to go into His presence. They had to be prepared. They could not just rush into His presence. When going into the presence of God we need to be prepared. What thoughts come to mind when we contemplate going into His presence? My sins, my unworthiness, my self-centeredness, the lusts of the mind and the flesh, the evil I would not, and the good I do not.

What about having communion and fellowship with God? How can we converse with God? How do we feel about being in His presence? These thoughts lead to other questions and thoughts. How can I be assured that God will be favorably disposed toward me? How can I go with boldness? How can I have freedom of entry? How can I have confidence?

There is only one answer: *by the faith of* (in) *Him* [Eph. 3:12]. By knowing that the Son of God has borne my sins, my guilt, and my punishment on the Cross, and shed His blood for me, personally. That is how I can go with boldness and confidence. There is no other way.

Then the question arises, how can we truly pray to God? *Let us therefore come boldly* (confidently) *unto the throne of grace, that we may obtain mercy, and find grace to help in time of need* [Heb. 4:16].

First, we must recognize and accept the fact that coming *boldly* (confidently) *unto the throne of grace* is not dependent upon our own emotions, moods, or feelings. When we begin to pray we must eliminate all such ideas or thoughts, because they are a hindrance to communicating with God. They are the work of the "evil one." We must recognize and accept the fact that prayer requires effort, discipline, and work.

Second, we are to remind ourselves of the basic truths of the Christian faith, and we are to live *in Christ* as members of the community of believers.

Third, God has provided a way for us to go into His presence. He has clothed us with the righteousness of Christ.

Fourth, we must remind ourselves of what we are doing and the reasons for those actions. The Apostle John provides additional light, saying,

> *But if we walk in the light, as he is in the light, we have fellowship one with another, and the blood of Jesus Christ his Son cleanseth us from all sin.*
> *If we say that we have no sin, we deceive ourselves, and the truth is not in us.*
> *If we confess our sins, he is faithful and just to forgive us our sins, and to cleanse us from all unrighteousness* [1 John 1:7–9].
>
> *My little children, these things write I unto you, that ye sin not* (may not sin). *And if any man sin, we have an advocate* (intercessor) *with the Father, Jesus Christ the righteous:*
> *And he is the propitiation for our sins: and not for ours only, but also for the sins of the whole world* [1 John 2:1–2].

Please note the sequence in these verses:

- *Fellowship one with another,*
- *Blood of Jesus Christ his Son cleanseth us,*
- *Say that we have no sin, we deceive ourselves,*

- *Truth is not in us,*
- *If we confess our sins, he is faithful,*
- *Forgive us our sins,*
- *Cleanse us from all unrighteousness,*
- *We have an advocate* (intercessor) *with the Father, and*
- *He is the propitiation for our sins.*

Then we state our belief in the Lord Jesus Christ and the revelations contained in Scripture.

Lastly, we thank God for all He has done. We thank Him for His love, mercy, justice, righteousness, compassion, Son, Word, Holy Spirit, and forgiveness. When we do this it is well to consider for a moment the Lord Jesus Christ and our salvation.

"In Christology the issue is not a change of our consciousness, but the transformation of the realm of lordship and thus of the very structure of life. Jesus Christ is not the object of our knowledge but the giver of new life. Therefore Christology is never just the 'knowledge of God the redeemer' but simultaneously the experience of a turning around in our existence," according to the insightful description provided by Otto Weber. This is a marvelous statement, and pray God it impacts us individually and collectively.

As we conclude our consideration of *boldness, access,* and *confidence,* it is beneficial to examine Calvin's teaching about Christ and our salvation, about doctrine and its application. Calvin, in simple, yet majestic language, glorifies the Lord Jesus Christ, His attributes, His virtues, and above all, His Deity, saying,

- "we see that our whole salvation and all its parts are comprehended in Christ,
- we should not derive the least portion from anywhere else,
- if we seek salvation, we are taught by the very name of Jesus, that it is of him.
- if we seek strength, it is in His dominion,
- if purity, in his conception,
- if gentleness, in His birth,

God's Riches and Power   59

- if we seek redemption, it is in His passion,
- if acquittal, in His condemnation,
- if remission of the curse, in His Cross,
- if satisfaction, in His sacrifice,
- if purification, in His blood,
- if reconciliation, in His descent into hell,
- if mortification of the flesh, in His tomb,
- if newness of life, in His resurrection,
- if immortality, in the same,
- if inheritance of the Heavenly Kingdom, in His entrance into Heaven,
- if protection, security, and an abundant supply of blessings, in His Kingdom,
- if untroubled expectation of judgment, in the power given to Him to judge."

It is all "in Him" and it is all "for us." Therefore, we can go with boldness and access into His presence with confidence.

Draw nigh (near) *to God, and He will draw nigh* (near) *to you* [Jas. 4:8]. When you do, you will realize His presence, you will have a sense of His glory and comfort, you will receive His strength and might, and you will know His love and kindness.

Paul began what we call the third chapter of Ephesians with the words *For this cause*, which referred back to the latter portion of the second chapter. Then he digresses in verses 2–13, which we have considered in detail, before returning to his initial thought. Once again, he uses the phrase *For this cause* and introduces the second great prayer in this letter.

Paul believed the Gospel was so wonderful that it was not possible for men to see its glory unless they were taught of God. Therefore, he told the followers at Ephesus that he continually prayed for God to give them

> ... *the spirit of wisdom and revelation in the knowledge of him:*
> (that) *the eyes of your understanding being enlightened; that ye may know what is the hope of his calling, and what* (are) *the riches of the glory of his inheritance in the saints* [Eph. 1:17–18].

Paul knew that spiritual illumination was necessary if one was to know the contents of the Gospel of our Lord Jesus Christ. Further, the Gospel reveals the eternal and invisible things that are beyond the normal comprehension of men.

His prayer in the first chapter of Ephesians is for revelation while the one in the third chapter is for realization and strength. Therefore, it is beneficial to compare the prayers in the first and third chapters. Consider the primary points of each one as presented by Ruth Paxson:

First Prayer 1:15–23	Second Prayer 3:14–21
Revelation	Realization
Enlightenment	Enablement
Light	Life
Know what you are	Be what you know
Know the Power of God	Experience the fullness of God
Ye in Christ	Christ in you
Christ's fullness in the Church	Church's fullness in Christ

We should know that the realization of Christ's abundant life in us is a process. The moment we are reborn, or have a new birth or new life, we become possessors of the fullness of Christ. However, this personal possession is a continuous and progressive process after the initial appropriation by faith.

It is important to realize and believe completely, that no matter how much of Christ's fullness we enjoy or experience today, there is always more tomorrow. Every tomorrow can bring ever greater fullness. The prayer for revelation in the first chapter contains a process introduced three times by the word *what* in verses eighteen and nineteen: *what is the hope of his calling, what* (are) *the riches of the glory of his inheritance in the saints, what is the exceeding greatness of his power to us-ward who believe* [Eph. 1:18–19]. The prayer for realization in the third chapter contains a process introduced by the word *that* on four occasions, as noted below,

> *That he would grant you, . . . to be strengthened with might by his Spirit in the inner man;*

> *That Christ may dwell in your hearts by faith; that ye, being rooted and grounded in love;*
> *May be able to comprehend (understand) with all saints what is the breadth (width), and length, and depth, and height;*
> *And to know the love of Christ, . . . that ye might be filled with all the fullness of God* [Eph. 3:16–19].

This prayer for realization may at first seem to be beyond reality, too great to grasp, and not understandable. However, the whole prayer must be considered and placed in the proper perspective. It is buttressed by two reassuring phrases, one objective and one subjective: *according to the riches of his glory* [Eph. 3:16] and *according to the power that worketh in us* [Eph. 3:20].

When considering the phrase, *according to the riches of his glory*, it is well to remember that God is not promising something He is unable to perform. He can do it. He knows His own resources and is able to bequeath His promises to His children. His plan for redemption is stable, practical, and workable. Further, all His riches are available to support it and carry it out. Nothing is omitted or held back.

Dr. Ironside describes it as follows: "The scripture says, 'according to,' not 'out of' His riches." He uses the illustration of a person contacting a millionaire requesting a donation for a worthy cause, and as a result he receives $100.00 or $1,000.00. He received the donation "out of the millionaire's riches." However, if he had received a number of signed blank checks, then he would have received "according to his riches."

God provides and we are to realize the riches of His glory through Jesus Christ crucified, risen, ascended, and glorified. He is our fullness and provides *according to* His riches.

Paul's prayer for the Ephesians is supported by the power that worketh in us. Our study of Ephesians reveals that we are heirs of God and joint heirs with Christ. Objectively we have grasped this truth, and doctrinally we believe it.

However, these facts present us with a problem. How do we become what we are meant to be and know what we should become? How can these *riches of his glory* be made to fit, so that we may live joyfully and triumphantly?

God's assurance of providing for our needs is evidenced by sending to us the Holy Spirit which was within the Lord Jesus Christ during His earthly ministry. Christ promised to send the Holy Spirit which He did at Pentecost. Ever since, He has been present in every member of His Body, the church, the community of believers. This is how we know what we are meant to be *according to the riches of his glory*, and know what we are to become *according to the power that worketh in us*.

May this exposition enable us to better understand,

> *That he would grant you, according to the riches of his glory, to be strengthened with might by his Spirit in the inner man;*
> *That Christ may dwell in your hearts by faith; that ye, being rooted and grounded in love,*
> *May be able to comprehend (understand) with all saints what is the breadth (width), and length, and depth, and height;*
> *And to know the love of Christ, which passeth knowledge, that ye might be filled with all the fulness of God* [Eph. 3:16–19].

It is according to the riches and the power of God that we realize that we are strengthened by His Spirit, that Christ dwells in our hearts, that we may comprehend and know the love of Christ, and that we might be filled with all the fullness of God.

Amen!

8

For This Cause

> *For this cause I bow my knees unto the Father of our Lord Jesus Christ,*
> *Of whom the whole family in heaven and earth is named, . . .*
> [Eph. 3:14–15].

There are a few observations to emphasize when examining the following:

> *For this cause I bow my knees unto the Father of our Lord Jesus Christ,*
> *Of whom the whole family in heaven and earth is named, ...*

The first thing to emphasize is that the Apostle is praying for the Ephesian followers, not for everyone in Ephesus. When he was writing to them and praying for them he was a prisoner. Even though he was, he could still pray. He might not be able to preach, or visit them, but he could pray for them.

Remember, no matter what condition or situation exists we can always pray and have communion with the Father through the Lord Jesus Christ. Paul's letters reveal he spent considerable time in prayer. He was active and he was interested even though his circumstances were unfavorable.

Second, the Apostle reminds us that prayer is as necessary as instruction. Please do not think Paul would not have been as fervent in his prayers if he had been free. He recognized the importance of prayer and was diligent in his prayers whether free or Christ's prisoner.

We need instruction and increased knowledge. Therefore, we are to read our Bibles and meditate upon various verses or thoughts. We read books, commentaries, or articles. We listen to lessons and sermons, we discuss them, and we study doctrine. All of this is important.

Paul realized the importance of instruction and that doctrine was essential. However, he also realized we should pray for ourselves and pray for enlightenment: pray that we may receive knowledge and instruction; pray that we may assimilate it and apply it; pray that it may grip our hearts and minds; and pray that we get self out of the way. Knowledge, instruction, and prayer always go together. They should never be separated.

Third, prayer is equally necessary in our dealings with others. Paul knew that the Ephesians would read, discuss, and study this Epistle. He knew that this teaching could not be made real to them without God's blessing and the power of the Holy Spirit. Paul knew that only as the Holy Spirit prepared them and opened their minds could they understand the truth and grasp it. That was reason enough to pray that their eyes of understanding might be enlightened.

We should learn a practical lesson from this. We must pray for people to be enlightened. It is not enough for instruction only. God uses prayer and the power of the Holy Spirit to enlighten people.

Fourth, we should note the way in which the Apostle prays. I am not talking about his physical position, but his internal position. He prays deliberately, neither haphazardly nor with little forethought.

There is a vital principle involved when considering this matter of prayer. It is not the posture or format that matter, but the attitude of worship, adoration, and praise. Regardless of the format or posture there is one thing that expresses itself loud and clear to God, the state of one's heart.

The attitude of the believer regarding prayer and going into the presence of God is not only important, it is revealing. Paul says two things concerning God's eternal purpose, our relationship to the Lord Jesus, and praying. First, Paul says, *In whom we have boldness and access with confidence by the faith of* (in) *him* (Christ) [Eph. 3:12]. Second, he says, *For this cause I bow my knees unto the Father of our Lord Jesus Christ* [Eph. 3:14]. This may seem to be a dichotomy, but it is not.

Please note that boldness, access, and confidence are followed by *I bow my knees unto the Father of our Lord Jesus Christ*. We may be bold and confident, but we are to bow our knees with a deep sense of humility. We have been chosen by God through the Lord Jesus, which provides us with boldness and access. But we are to remember with most grateful hearts that when we pray we are going into the presence of God and communing with Him. What a privilege and honor has been bestowed upon us by God's grace!

This should remind us that boldness means neither brazenness nor presumption. Confidence means neither audacity nor effrontery. Further, we should not pray with an easy, glib familiarity. That is a denial of what is taught throughout Scripture. Some attitudes about prayer are based upon either ignorance of Scripture or God, or both. Paul knew the way into the presence of God. Yet he says, *I bow my knees*. He knew the One he was approaching.

Paul's prayer is a marvelous example of how we should pray: bowing unto the Father; praying for others; Christ dwelling in our hearts; being rooted and grounded in love; comprehending with all the saints; knowing the love of Christ; and being filled with the fullness of God.

Remember, Paul is praying for converted pagans, for people who had been or still were slaves, for people who were educated or uneducated. However, because they were followers *in Christ* he offers this prayer. He wanted them to reach the highest levels of the Christian experience that is possible in the world. He knew these things were the key to truly living a life *in Christ*. He prayed that they could grasp it by the might and power of the Spirit dwelling in the inner man.

What Paul does not pray for is just as important as what he prays for. He does not pray for a change in either their circumstances or his, he does not pray for his release from prison, and he does not offer some general prayer. What characterizes Paul's prayer?

First, it is spiritual in its content, it is not about material things. You will recall at the beginning of this wonderful letter the Apostle says, *Blessed be the God and Father of our Lord Jesus Christ, who hath blessed us with all spiritual blessings in heavenly places in Christ* [Eph. 1:3]. Paul prays that we *might be filled with the knowledge of his will in all wisdom and spiritual understanding* [Col. 1:9]. Paul's entire attitude toward life is one of the Spirit; therefore, he begins with the Spirit.

What did the Lord Jesus teach? . . . *seek ye first the kingdom of God, and his righteousness; and all these things shall be added unto you* [Matt. 6:33].

Second, it is a specific prayer. He singles out specific items or needs and enumerates them one by one. Please note that he is neither vague nor haphazard in his prayers. Paul is not concerned about the beauty of the language, but with the outpouring of God's spiritual blessings through the Holy Spirit.

Again and again Paul's primary concerns in prayer are spiritual growth and development, knowledge of God, relationship to God and Christ, and enjoying the Father, Son, and Holy Ghost. These should also be our primary concerns.

Paul does not make light of the problems involved in living our daily lives, nor does the New Testament make light of them. Scripture neither minimizes nor ignores a difficulty or a problem. It faces them. It does not promise that the problem, difficulty, or condition will be removed easily or quickly, because Scripture is realistic. This truth is a key to understanding Paul's prayer.

What does the New Testament say?

> *In the world ye shall have tribulation: but be of good cheer; I have overcome the world* [John 16:33].

> *Confirming* (strengthening) *the souls of the disciples, and exhorting them to continue in the faith, and that we must through much tribulation enter into the kingdom of God* [Acts 14:22].

> *For unto you it is given in the behalf of Christ, not only to believe on him, but also to suffer for his sake* [Phil. 1:29].

> *Yea, and all that will live godly in Christ Jesus shall suffer persecution* [2 Tim. 3:12].

The Book of Revelation contains prophecies of trials, troubles, and tribulations.

There is nothing in the New Testament that suggests all our difficulties are going to be removed by some magic wand and that everything is going to be wonderful during our lives in this world. The New Testament realistically helps us to meet situations, to overcome them, and to be *more than conquerors through him that loved us* [Rom. 8:37]. The Bible reveals that because there is sin in the world (and in us) there will be trials, troubles, problems, difficulties, and tribulations.

People in most categories believe it is within man's capability to get everything in order in this world. They believe that the only requirements for so doing are time and money, and given enough of both an idyllic, utopian society will emerge, peace will reign, and difficulties will disappear.

These people do not realize that sin in the human breast and heart is a reality that must be addressed. It causes wars, discords, and troubles. The Bible recognizes and realizes that the true cause of all the problems besetting man collectively and individually is sin, and it should neither be ignored nor minimized.

Paul does not pray for a certain method to resolve these problems, difficulties, and situations. The Apostle's method is to pray that in facing these obstacles we turn to God, and that according to His riches, we will be strengthened with might by His Spirit in the inner man.

Oh, pray God that we can learn that no matter what besets us, if we first turn to God the inner man will be strengthened.

What does our Lord say about this? *And he* (Jesus) *spake a parable unto to them to this end, that men ought always to pray, and not to faint* (lose heart) [Luke 18:1].

If you want to avoid fainting and falling, then pray. "Prayer . . . is to fill the lungs of the soul with the oxygen of the Holy Spirit and His power. If you want to stand on your feet and not to falter fill yourself with the life of God," according to the wonderful, uplifting, spirit-filled words of Martyn Lloyd-Jones.

To paraphrase this, we should not expend our energy or waste our time contemplating the things that tend to defeat us, but we should utilize our energy in building ourselves up. This is the only way to appreciate what it is to rejoice in tribulation.

Therefore, we are to remember Paul's admonition to the Corinthians,

> *We are troubled* (hard pressed) *on every side, yet not distressed* (crushed); *we are perplexed, but not in despair;*
> *Persecuted, but not forsaken; cast* (struck) *down, but not destroyed;*
> *Always bearing about in the body the dying of the Lord Jesus, that the life also of Jesus might be made manifest in our body* [2 Cor. 4:8–10].

Paul describes relatively common maladies that affect people and tells them what they are to do and not do.

The renowned theologian, John Calvin, offers comfort and strength for the troubles and hard pressed conditions we encounter as we walk along life's pathway. He addresses these unfavorable situations, as we call them, with straight from the shoulder talk saying, ". . . by way of explanation, to show that his abject condition, so far from detracting from God's glory, rather serves to advance it. 'For', he says 'we are reduced to straits but at length the Lord opens a way of escape; we are oppressed with poverty, but the Lord comes to our aid. Many foes are in arms against us but in God's keeping we are safe. In a word, though we are brought so low that all seems over with us, yet we do not perish.' The last possibility he mentions is the most serious of all. You see how he turns to his own advantage every charge that the wicked bring against him."

O' the insight and positive approach that Calvin provides in the time of trouble. He had learned from his encounters with Satan and Satan's minions that he would face continuous assaults as he served the Lord Jesus. He came to the realization that Jesus was not only his refuge, but his strength, his wisdom, and his armor. Therefore, Paul knew (and we should know) in whom he trusted, the Lord Jesus Christ. May we be able to say with the Apostle Paul, *Nay, in all these things we are more than conquerors through him that loved us* [Rom. 8:37]

The principle involved should be obvious to one and all. It means recognizing the source and taking appropriate action. Proverbs succinctly gets to the core of the matter.

> *For as he thinketh in his heart, so is he* [Prov. 23:7].
>
> *Keep thy heart with all diligence; for out of it are the issues of life* [Prov. 4:23].

What does our Lord say? When Jesus was with His disciples after telling a parable, He said,

> *There is nothing from without* (outside) *a man, that . . . can defile him: but the things which come out of him, they . . . defile the man.*
> *For from within, out of the heart of men, proceed evil thoughts, adulteries, fornications, murders,*
> *Thefts, covetousness, wickedness, deceit, lasciviousness* (licentiousness), *an evil eye, blasphemy, pride, foolishness:*
> *All these evil things come from within, and defile the man* [Mark 7:15, 21–23].

It is interesting to note what Jesus did not say about the things that defile a man. He did not attribute the cause for a person's acts or conditions to other people or to the culture of the society. That is quite different from what we hear today. Today, people want to place the blame for a person being defiled on that which enters into him or her, not that which comes from within, *out of the heart of men.*

Our Lord aptly stated it is not the temptations that meet us on the street, or in our offices or homes, that determine our actions and conduct. It is in the heart of the man who faces the temptations. Two men can face the same conditions; one falls, the other stands. The difference is not in the temptation, but in the response of the individual's heart.

Therefore, we must look at the inner man. Yes, there is an inner man, an inner person. It includes the heart, the mind, the soul, and the spirit. It is *in Christ.* Paul means by the *inner man* our central and highest form of life, and he prays that it may be strengthened. It is the opposite of the outward body with all its facilities and functions.

Life is a mystery in both its lowest and loftiest forms and is composed of many facets and variations—physical, intellectual, and spiritual.

We can say that a person's physical life is energetic, but that does not mean the individual has great muscular force, or ability. It describes something beneath the physical surface that inspires the whole.

A person's intellectual life may be described as strong or weak. This does not mean that a particular faculty or ability is admirable or not. A particular faculty may be strong or feeble yet the overall assessment may be the opposite. The center of the person's intellectual energy may be different from that of another faculty.

A person's spiritual life may have certain imperfections. A particular faculty may be strong or vigorous, but the central core may be weak. Some exhibit certain strengths, but a closer examination reveals the lack of spiritual strength. Others may seem to aspire for Christian perfection, but they have neither staying power, nor real vigor. Others may have a keen understanding of certain Biblical truths or doctrine, but they are weak. Others seem capable of great devotion, yet give the impression they are wanting in spiritual energy.

In each of these cases the energy or vigor is not derived from the central fountain of life but from springs that are removed from the center. Therefore, they need *to be strengthened with might by His spirit in the inner man* [Eph. 3:16].

Our secret as followers *in Christ* is that we have the *inner man.* When the *inner man* has been strengthened by the Holy Spirit, then what happens around and about us and even to our outward being is relatively unimportant. May God assure us of possessing the *inner man* and being a new creature in Christ Jesus.

The question may be asked: What happens to us when we are strengthened by the Spirit in the inner man? We learn that apart from Christ we can do nothing, and that *in Christ* all things are possible. We also learn when we live in the light of God and His Word that we hunger and thirst after righteousness, old things fade away, and the new light attracts us.

Christ brings through the Spirit a clearer knowledge of God and our responsibilities, including a firmer resolve to obey His commands; a more generous heart for others and the desire for fellowship with Christ; more intense delight in righteousness and justice; deeper joy in the love of God; and more vivid hope of immortality. These things come through the power working in us *according to the riches of his glory* [Eph. 3:16].

There are several interesting points to ponder at this time: our relations with Christ are neither passive, nor stationary. If He is to *abide* in us, we must *abide* in Him, He first comes to us because of His infinite grace and mercy but, and I say this reverently, He does not make His home with us unless we have the strength and will to detain Him. We may be conscious that He comes to us and blesses us, but then we have the feeling that we do not have a firm grasp of Him. He comes, but we let Him go. We do not bring Him in to stay with us. We do not grasp hold. We do not stay connected.

The Apostle states in the next verse *That Christ may dwell in your hearts by faith* [Eph. 3:17]. We have noted that the Apostle's mind is orderly and proceeds logically step-by-step. Note the sequence of his prayer: *That he would grant you, according to the riches of His glory, to be strengthened with might by his Spirit in the inner man; That Christ may dwell in your hearts by faith* [Eph. 3:16–17].

We have to be strengthened for Him to dwell in us by faith. It is a result of the Spirit working within the inner man and impacting the reason, will, conscience, memory, hope, love, reverence, awe, joy, and gratitude by blending them into a strong, vibrant faith. Yes, it is true that apart from Christ we have no real strength. We can have access to His life, righteousness, and peace before we are strong, while we are yet babes in the faith. However, His power and the grace of the Holy Spirit cannot come upon us apart from Himself.

Paul focuses our attention on something far greater than an initial awareness of union with Christ. He is leading us to Christ dwelling in our hearts. The Greek word for *dwell* in the seventeenth verse is *katoikeō*, which means "to settle down," "to dwell fixedly in a place," and "the indwelling of Christ."

The emphasis is on the word *dwell*. This is accomplished only by the abiding presence of Christ in one's heart and great faith. Where there is great faith there must be great strength. This strength is given to the inner man by the power of the Spirit.

Paul prays that the Ephesians (and we) may receive by the Spirit the permanent presence of Christ in our hearts, which is rooted and grounded in love.

Amen!

9

Strengthening Believers

> *That he would grant you, according to the riches of his glory, to be strengthened with might by his Spirit in the inner man;*
> *That Christ may dwell in your hearts by faith; that ye, being rooted and grounded in love,*
> *May be able to comprehend (understand) with all saints what is the breadth (width), and length, and depth, and height;*
> *And to know the love of Christ, which passeth knowledge, that ye might be filled with all the fullness of God* [Eph. 3:16–19].

The Apostle prays for the inner man to be strengthened with might by the Holy Spirit. He prays for those who are members of the community of believers. Paul prayed for these people in the first chapter, and he prays for them again in the third chapter.

He prays for specific items: that the believers will be *strengthened with might by his Spirit;* that Christ *may dwell in your hearts by faith; that ye, being rooted and grounded in love,* they will *comprehend* (understand) *with all saints, know the love of Christ, and be filled with all the fullness of God.* These are fantastic, mind-boggling items. They should cause us to stop and take notice.

Why do I say this? Because often times these great blessings are not considered together, nor is sufficient emphasis placed upon them individually. Consequently, the Holy Spirit does not expound upon these wonderful truths in our hearts and our minds. Sometimes we do not hunger and thirst after righteousness. As a result, the seed does not have the proper nutrients in order to germinate and to grow.

Some people think they have received a sufficient portion of God's grace, when in reality they have not tasted or experienced the best part but have been only exposed to a little morsel. Paul wants them to know and to enjoy the full measure.

This point needs to be emphasized because Paul knew that forgiveness and the promise of salvation were only the beginning of a follower's life *in Christ*. It is only the first step. It merely indicates the beginning of the life *in Christ*. It is like going to the first grade and staying there for three score and ten years. By doing so, the rewards, riches, joy, and strength of receiving an education are forfeited.

Unfortunately, many members of the community of believers stop at the first grade. They are merely concerned about their personal security and safety. They believe if they do that much, God, through Christ, will cling to them. They do not even realize their need for His available strength.

Their only concern is to belong to the kingdom, to gain entrance, and to pay the minimum dues. They want to have some assurance that their sins are forgiven and that they will not go to hell, or their version of it. They want the hope of going to heaven on some basis. Therefore, they have an initial experience, decide that that is it, and rest upon it.

These people never grow, and you cannot detect any appreciable difference in them ten, twenty-five, or fifty years later. They are content where they are, and think they have everything. They are not developing, but they are in danger of losing the little they do have, since they do not have the strength or desire to grasp it and to take hold.

Their status or condition is very different from what we find in Paul's prayer for the Ephesian followers *in Christ*. Paul prays that Christ may dwell in their hearts and that they may know the fullness of God. His prayer indicates what is possible for all the members of the community of believers, not just a few. Charles Spurgeon, the great preacher of the nineteenth century, once said, "There is a point in grace as much above the ordinary Christian as the ordinary Christian is above the worldling." He is saying that there is a stage in the life *in Christ* that has developed to the point that it is above and beyond the ordinary follower as he or she is above the person of the secular world.

The person *in Christ* is on a higher level or plane than the non-follower. Spurgeon makes us aware of the fact that the person *in Christ* is on a higher plane than the natural man or the non-Christian. We must accept this teaching if we believe that Christ can dwell in our hearts, that we can know both God's love and Christ's love, and that God's fullness may fill us.

There are several questions to ponder. Have we reached the level to which Spurgeon refers? Does Christ dwell in our hearts by faith? Do we really know God the Father, who is able to do exceedingly abundantly beyond all we ask or think? Do we think we can rest on our oars and that there is nothing more to do? How can we reach the higher level? There is only one answer to all these questions. We must *be strengthened with might by His spirit in the inner man.* Therefore, the question needs to be asked: why does the inner man need to be strengthened?

The first response to consider is that initially the follower *in Christ* is only a babe. A babe has only started to live, is not fully developed, and needs to be strengthened.

> *And I, brethren, could not speak unto you as unto spiritual, but as unto carnal, even as unto babes in Christ* [1 Cor. 3:1].

What is true of a babe? It is weak, ignorant, undeveloped, immature, and innocent; it lacks immunity, needs protection, views things superficially, does not know the ugly things of the world, and does not know that dangers are present.

The same may be said for the teenager or adult who comes to know Christ and joins a church with certain expectations. These people may feel they will never have another problem, and that everything will be solved. In their innocence, they may believe there will never be a cloud or storm in their lives. They need to be strengthened so that they will be able to endure pain or misfortune.

> *I write unto you, little children, because your sins are forgiven you for his name's sake.*
> *I write unto you, fathers, because ye have known him that is from the beginning. I write unto you, young men, because ye have overcome the wicked one. I write unto you, little children, because ye have known the Father*
> *I have written unto you, fathers, because ye have known him that is from the beginning. I have written unto you, young men, because ye are strong, and the word of God abideth in you, and ye have overcome the wicked one* [1 John 2:12–14].

John writes to the little children, fathers, and young men. He writes to the different gradations.

A second reason for strengthening the inner man is the existence of the devil, the adversary, the accuser of the brethren. The Greek word *diabolos* is interpreted as "devil" in certain portions of the New Testament, and it means "accuser." Regarding the devil, Peter admonishes us to *Be sober, be vigilant; because your adversary the devil, as a roaring lion, walketh about, seeking whom he may devour* [1 Pet. 5:8].

The inimitable John Calvin focuses attention on our primary adversary with simple, dynamic words when he says regarding the command to *Be sober*. This explanation extends further, to the extent that as we are at war with a most fierce and most powerful enemy, we are to be strenuous in resisting him. He uses a twofold metaphor, that they were to be sober, and that they were to be watchful. . . . those who indulge in earthly cares and pleasures think of nothing else, (although) oppressed as they are by spiritual lethargy.

He (Peter) says that we must carry on a warfare in this world, and reminds us that we are not dealing with a common enemy, but with one who, like a lion, runs here and there, *seeking whom he may devour*. He concludes from this that we ought to watch carefully. Peter encourages us . . . he says that we have a contest not with flesh and blood, but with spiritual wickedness, etc. . . . We too often turn peace into sloth, . . . because we indulge ourselves according to the will of the flesh, as though we were beyond the reach of danger.

He compares the devil to a lion, as though he were saying that he is a savage wild beast. . . . He calls him the adversary of the godly, so that they know that they worship God and profess faith in Christ on the condition that they have a continual warfare with the devil, for he who fights with the Head (Christ) will not spare the members.

"Paul says the real problem is the struggle against the principalities and powers. Therefore, the inner man needs to be strengthened, because this power that confronts him is great, subtle, devious, and cunning. The devil is not only an accuser, he is an adversary, and as an adversary he can turn himself into an angel of light, as Paul noted when saying that this is *no marvel; for Satan himself is transformed* (transforms himself) *into an angel of light* [2 Cor. 11:14]. He can quote Scripture, reason, rationalize, present arguments and cases, and appear to describe or discuss a truth, but he will lead you astray," as forcefully stated by Martyn Lloyd-Jones.

Considering the various wiles of the evil one, or devil, provides powerful reasons for strengthening oneself to repel this formidable foe, through the Word and by the power of the Holy Spirit.

The devil makes a special effort to attack the inner man. Unfortunately, there is much emphasis on the sins of the flesh and relatively little attention focused on the lusts of the mind or heart. Consequently, people are not cognizant of the subtleties or attacks that can be made upon the inner man by various means and methods. The evil one may ignore the outward person and concentrate upon the inner one. Solomon proclaims a great truth when he says, *Keep thy heart with all diligence; for out of it are the issues of life* [Prov. 4:23].

Third, the reason for strengthening the inner man is the greatness of what is offered and the possibilities for us: that Christ may dwell in our hearts by faith; that we may know the love of God; and that we may be filled with all the fullness of God. These possibilities require being strengthened in order to receive them and deal with the ordeals and temptations of life.

Some people may ask, why do we need to be strengthened in order to receive life or light? They infer it is odd that someone would have to be strengthened to receive Jesus Christ fully and completely.

Why do we need to be strengthened to receive the Lord Jesus Christ? On the surface it seems quite ridiculous. However, Paul prays that we will be strengthened with might by His Spirit (God's Spirit). Some say, if Christ is our strength, why do we need strength to receive Him?

During World War II people were lost at sea or were prisoners in concentration camps. When they were rescued or set free, there were many people who wanted to make sure they received a banquet. However, such an event resulted in the deaths of some that were rescued or freed.

Why? Because they were not strong enough to partake of such food. Before a person in a weakened condition can take much food, he must be strengthened. Before a person can ingest a heavy meal, he or she must concentrate on regaining strength.

The Apostle prays for the disciples to be strengthened. He prays for the Ephesians to be strengthened in order for them to become strong and mighty, and to receive Christ in their hearts and detain Him.

What does Scripture say about this?

> *I have fed you with milk, and not with meat* (solid food): *for hitherto* (until now) *ye were not able to bear it, neither yet now are ye able* [1 Cor. 3:2].
>
> *For when for the time* (though by this time) *ye ought to be teachers, ye have need that one teach you again which be the first principles of the oracles* (sayings) *of God; and are become such as have need of milk, and not of strong meat* (solid food).
> *For every one that useth* (partakes of) *milk is unskillful in the word of righteousness: for he is a babe.*
> *But strong meat* (solid food) *belongeth to them that are of full age* (mature), *even those who by reason of use* (practice) *have their senses exercised* (trained) *to discern both good and evil* [Heb. 5:12–14].

The author of this Epistle goads the Hebrews in order to prod them out of their lethargy. He says they ought to be ashamed that they are still in the primary classes in school when they ought to be teachers. However, instead of being teachers, they are not even good pupils who can grasp the basic teachings of God and the elementary principles of Christianity.

"We must learn from the whole of life, because the truly wise man is the one who knows how far short he comes of any complete understanding," according to the renowned theologian John Calvin. We are to progress as we learn and not remain at the beginning forever. Note what Isaiah says, *Whom shall he teach knowledge? and whom shall he make to understand doctrine* (the message)? *them that are* (just) *weaned from the milk, and* (just) *drawn from the breasts* [Isa. 28:9].

We will spend our days in the elementary classes if we do not exert the energy to learn but remain lazy or indolent. It is each person's duty to pass on knowledge and understanding so that it may be used for mutual edification.

Such as have need of milk [Heb. 5:12]. The author is saying this because they are carnal; they cannot digest solid food. Milk is the food or teaching with which the babes in the faith, or the ignorant, begin. Paul says, *Brethren, be not children in understanding: howbeit in malice be ye children* (babes), *but in understanding be men* (mature) [1 Cor. 14:20]. Paul remonstrates those who cannot receive the more advanced teaching by calling them children.

The true purpose behind teaching and learning is to enable us to grow and mature into adults in the faith, so that we will not be tossed about by every wind of doctrine. This teaching was important to the Apostle Paul. He stressed it to the Ephesians. He told them that God *gave some, apostles; and some, prophets; and some, evangelists; and some, pastors and teachers* [Eph. 4:11].

What does Paul want the Ephesians to become? He explains it simply and forcefully, saying, *That we henceforth be no more children, tossed to and fro, and carried about with every wind of doctrine, by the sleight* (trickery) *of men, and cunning craftiness, whereby they lie in wait to deceive* [Eph. 4:14].

Paul knew the importance of maturing in the faith. He knew that knowledge was a key element in growing in the faith. He did not want the devil to beguile and devour a single person. Therefore, he admonishes the followers *in Christ* to grow in knowledge and in faith.

Naturally, we must exhibit indulgence to those who are really children or to those who are just beginning to know Christ. But, "Anyone who ought to grow with time (it) is inexcusable if he remains forever a child," as appropriately expressed by John Calvin. The infant is nourished by milk in order that it may be gradually weaned to stronger food.

The writer to the Hebrews is not referring to how we are justified, but is speaking in a simpler sense of the fullness of knowledge, which leads to perfection. Paul says, *whom we preach, warning every man, and teaching every man in all wisdom; that we may present every man perfect in Christ Jesus* [Col. 1:28].

Under the influence of the Holy Spirit, Paul says "that those who indulge their ignorance are blocked from obtaining a genuine knowledge of Christ. The teaching of the Gospel does not bear fruit in them because they do not come close to reaching the goal," according to John Calvin.

God wants the followers *in Christ*, the Christians, as Calvin declares, "to develop the ability to discern good and evil. Only when they are properly instructed in the truth do they have protection against Satan's falsehoods. . . . A faith that wavers between truth and falsehood is liable to collapse at any time."

The author of Hebrews states that all the senses must be capable of discerning both good and evil, as noted in his letter where he says, *even those who by reason of use* (practice) *have their senses exercised* (trained) *to discern both good and evil* [Heb. 5:14]. When we neglect the discipline of learning, then we do not have sufficient capabilities to discern or we lack them completely.

Calvin "maintain[s] that it is easy to judge the spirit that actuates those who scarcely allow men to touch (or who refuse through ignorance or obstinacy) what the apostle bids them handle constantly; who pretend that the neglect which is here so severely reproved is in fact praiseworthy: who take away the Word of God, the only rule of true discernment, which is declared here to be a necessity for all Christians. Even among those who have been freed from that devilish prohibition and who enjoy the freedom to learn there is nonetheless an indifference both to hearing and to reading. When we neglect this discipline we are senseless and void of all discernment."

How is the weakness in the inner man exhibited? First, in a spiritual sense the mind needs to be strengthened. This is necessary if we are to successfully combat doubts, dullness or the inability to think clearly, trouble brought about by our imagination, evil thoughts, or a wandering mind when trying to read, study Scripture, and pray.

Our minds need to be strengthened when reading and studying the Word of God. The Epistle to the Ephesians is not simple, nor are the other books of the Bible. You cannot grasp it in a casual manner. You cannot race through it. You cannot take it on the run.

People may say sincerely that they do not understand Scripture. Probably, the reason is that their minds need to be strengthened. We are meant to apprehend the truths of God, and cannot do so unless our minds are strengthened.

"There are people who do not know or realize this. Some say they do not want to know what Scripture says. Some say, 'I am a simple Christian'; 'I am a plain person'; 'I do practical things'; 'I work'; 'I give my witness'; 'I cannot grapple with doctrine and theology, nor do I need to,'" according to Martyn Lloyd-Jones

However, we are to make the effort to understand the New Testament teachings. We are meant to understand them and to exercise our responsibility. Not to make the effort to understand the teachings of God and Christ is to deny Scripture.

Intellectual lethargy is probably the greatest sin of many members of the community of believers today. Too many are content to recount their early experiences with their primary level of learning, or to base everything on their carnal knowledge. They remain where they began. They do not come to know the unsearchable riches of God's holy truth. Therefore, Paul prays that their minds might be strengthened in order that they may realize the great possibilities of the life *in Christ* and rejoice in them. Then to bear witness and testimony to the glory of God.

Second, our hearts need to be strengthened. The Psalmists cries:

> *Teach me thy way, O Lord; I will walk in thy truth: unite my heart* (give me singleness of heart) *to fear* (have reverential awe for) *thy name.*
> *I will praise thee, O Lord my God, with all my heart: and I will glorify thy name for evermore* [Ps. 86:11–12].

The heart can be divided. It needs to be strengthened and united by the Holy Spirit.

Third, our will needs to be strengthened. At times it is feeble and irresolute. We need to recognize this and accept it. When we resolve, or desire, to do good then we need the strength of the Holy Spirit to fortify our wills. The Apostle prays that the inner man may be strengthened by the power of the Holy Spirit and that God may grant, give, or bestow a free gift upon you so that you might be strengthened.

How are we to be strengthened? According to the riches of His glory and by all the attributes of God—His might, His majesty, His holiness, His purity, His righteousness, His justice, His total being, and His Holy Spirit. It is the function of the Holy Spirit to do this. The Spirit convicts us of sin, gives us the gift of faith, and strengthens us.

The Apostle's prayer is most appropriate for today and the times in which we live.

Amen!

10

The Spirit of Christ

> *That Christ may dwell in your hearts by faith; that ye, being rooted and grounded in love,* . . . [Eph. 3:17].

What a wonderful, heartwarming, uplifting statement: *That Christ may dwell in your hearts by faith.* The Apostle is writing to and praying for the Ephesian members of the community of believers. He assumes that they will understand his letter and that they will be strengthened with might by the Holy Spirit.

Paul's statement that *Christ may dwell* ". . . does not satisfy Christ's heart, nor fulfill God's purpose. When God exalted His Son to be Head over the church, He gave Him the right to become the Lord over every Christian. The word "dwell" connotes the fixed, permanent abode of the one who owns; it is illuminated and interpreted by Paul's other word, "To me to live is Christ." This word "dwell" makes the human personality of the Christian the home of Christ into which he may settle down and be absolutely at home, possessing, controlling and using it as He wills. He is to be the presiding Presence, permeating and possessing all.

"*In your hearts*, (speaks directly to each of us and signifies that) [i]n the innermost sanctuary Christ is to be given the place of pre-eminence, enshrined and enthroned as Lord over all," as appropriately described by Ruth Paxson.

For *Christ to dwell in our hearts* means that we must respond in faith to the Word of God and Christ's teachings. This means that on our part there must be "the willing yielding of the Christian to Christ's possession and upon the appropriation of Christ Himself by faith," as Paxson declares.

Peter says in his second letter, *But grow in grace, and in the knowledge of our Lord and Saviour Jesus Christ* [2 Pet. 3:18]. The Apostle Paul says we are to be *no more children, tossed to and fro, and carried about with every wind of doctrine* [Eph. 4:14]. We are to discipline ourselves and grow in the knowledge of doctrine and the Lord Jesus Christ.

Paul prays that the followers may be strengthened and that Christ may dwell in their hearts. The Apostle is not praying that they become Christians, or praying for their conversion, salvation, and justification. He is praying that Christ may dwell in their hearts. You cannot be a member of the community of believers, or a Christian, without Christ being in you and you being *in Christ*.

Paul knew the Ephesian followers belonged, but he prayed that Christ may dwell in their hearts.

> *But ye are not in the flesh, but in the Spirit, if so be that the Spirit of God dwell in you. Now if any man have not the Spirit of Christ, he is none of his* [Rom. 8:9].

"This passage also teaches us that by the word *Spirit* Paul has not up to this point meant the *mind* or the *understanding*, which the advocates of free will call the superior part of the soul, but the gift of heaven. He explains that it is those whom God governs by His Spirit who are spiritual, and not those who obey reason on their own impulse.

"Those in whom the Spirit does not reign do not belong to Christ; therefore, those who serve the flesh are not Christians, for those who separate Christ from His Spirit make Him like a dead image or a corpse.

"We must either deny Christ, or confess that we become Christians by His Spirit. It is dreadful indeed to hear that men have so departed from the Word of the Lord, that they not only boast that they are Christians without the Spirit of God but also ridicule the faith of others," as expressed by John Calvin.

Illustrations of this same desire are provided by our Lord Jesus Christ.

In the Book of Revelation, the Lord Jesus addresses His followers, recognizing they have a relationship with Him but they are not controlled by Him, which is a significant difference. They are lukewarm (neither hot nor cold). They have dealings with Christ, but He is not the focal point of their lives. They need to strengthen themselves for increased dealings and dependence upon Christ and to be habitations for Him through the Spirit [Rev. 3:14–22].

In John's Gospel, Jesus, while talking to His followers, says He is going to leave them, but in another sense He is coming unto them. When He spoke to them they were already His followers, but the Comforter would come to be with them. Jesus also emphasizes that He will not manifest Himself to the world, but only to those who are His followers and who, as He says, *hath my commandments, and keepeth them, he it is that loveth me: and he that loveth me shall be loved of my Father, and I will love him, and will manifest* (reveal) *myself to him* [John 14:21].

That is a revealing and strong statement. As the saying goes, it draws a line in the sand. Note what Jesus says immediately thereafter: *If a man love me, he will keep my words: and my Father will love him, and we will come unto him, and make our abode* (home) *with him* [John 14:23]. These words by the Master are tough but true. They are not for the meek and mild.

There is a distinct difference between believing in Christ and having Christ dwell in your heart and mind. To believe in the Lord Jesus Christ is not the end of Christianity. On the contrary, it is only the beginning. It is absolutely essential to believe the truth about His person and His work.

When Christ manifests Himself to us, then He becomes a real person. That is what happened to Paul on the road to Damascus and in the days following. That is what happens to us.

> *To reveal his Son in me, that I might preach him among the heathen* (Gentiles); *immediately I conferred not with flesh and blood* [Gal. 1:16].

Paul says, *To reveal his Son in me*. It does not say "to me," but *in me*. It is an inward manifestation of the Lord Jesus, in which He is made as real unto us any other person we may know.

Hudson Taylor said it so beautifully,

> Lord Jesus, make thyself to me,
> *A living bright reality;*
> *More present to faith's vision,*
> *More keen than any outward object seen;*
> *More dear, more intimately nigh,*
> Than e'en the sweetest earthly tie.

We are to be united to Christ. He is to become our center, our focal point. He is to become not only real, but well-known to us. We are to have a personal knowledge of our Lord Jesus Christ. We are to take this even further. Christ's presence in our hearts, yours and mine, is real, not make-believe. Christ is present through the Holy Spirit: He influences us and bestows His grace upon us in ways we may not understand fully. However, He can and will dwell within us. The Apostle Paul says, *What? know ye not that your body is the temple of the Holy Ghost which is in you, which ye have of God, and ye are not your own* [1 Cor. 6:19]? In this verse, Paul reprimands the Corinthian followers in the Way and wants them to stay away from the sins of the flesh and filthiness.

He tells them forthrightly that their bodies are temples of the Holy Spirit and that they are not under their own jurisdiction, but under God's, because He has acquired them.

Paul, under the influence of the Holy Spirit, places a special emphasis on this fact by using the word *temple*, since the Spirit of God cannot be in an unclean place. Have you really thought of the great honor God bestows upon us by wanting His Spirit to dwell within us? Likewise, we should want the Spirit to dwell within us.

Second, Scripture says, *and ye are not your own*. We are not under our own authority, and we are not to live as we want. We are to live as God wants. Why? Because as Paul says, *For to this end Christ both died, and rose, and revived* (lived again), *that he might be Lord both of the dead and living* [Rom. 14:9]. In addition, Peter says,

> *Forasmuch as ye know that ye were not redeemed with corruptible* (perishable) *things, as silver and gold, from your vain conversation* (aimless conduct) *received by tradition from your fathers;*
> *But with the precious blood of Christ, as of a lamb without blemish and without spot* [1 Pet. 1:18–19].

When Paul says "body," he means our physical frame. He is referring to the fact that Christ Himself is in you, not just His influence.

How does this happen? How does it become possible? By faith! *That Christ may dwell in your hearts by faith*. Faith reveals this to us. It is possible to read Scripture with intellectual understanding, but without faith the Scriptures may be read without grasping their true meaning.

It is possible to read this portion of the third chapter without realizing Christ will come right into your heart, and you will know Him as a living reality. The person lacking faith will not know this.

Faith enables us to read Scripture, to hear it, to know that it is God's Word, and to realize that it is God who is speaking. Faith enables a person to believe God's Word, to fully accept it, and to depend upon it. When a person comes to believe it, then he begins to pray for it.

Paul prays for the elect at Ephesus that they might be *strengthened with might by His Spirit* [Eph. 3:16]. Paul experienced it and believed it. Therefore, he wanted the followers at Ephesus to do the same.

In order to put these words, *To be strengthened with might* in the proper perspective, it is prudent to consider Ruth Paxson's exposition as she states, "Is there any greater need in the Christian's life than to be made strong and with a power outside of himself? How often he feels that he is going backward rather than forward. He is conscious of weakness, failures, defeats, and backslidings that are well-nigh overpowering. More than once he cries out in anguish of spirit, 'Is it worth while to try to keep on? I just have not the strength for this conflict.' Nor has he, and God rejoices whenever a child of his comes to the end of himself and acknowledges his own utter impotency, for then God can begin to work. The Pentecost promise was for power. We are to be made strong with power through a Person, (Christ Jesus).

"The Holy Spirit who worked for us to implant life now works in us to impart power. He lives within us to strengthen and energize us with divine might and by a definite and continuous process. The life bestowed by the Spirit through rebirth is realized in fullness through Renewal."

Like Paul, we should pray and go on praying in faith until we really know Him. Then we should continue to pray that he will dwell within us and that we will know more and more of His unsearchable riches.

This great prayer of Paul's is not easy to expound, or to understand on the surface or through a cursory reading. There are great treasures and truths in it. They must be searched out and examined. Our faith in Christ can, in a sense, be compared to an ocean. A small child can play on the beach and splash in the water as the waves gently break on the sand. However, a great ship can be tossed to and fro by mighty waves in the middle of the ocean. Also, the ocean can reveal unlimited information if one will probe and seek it in that vast storehouse. We are to search and search, and fully enjoy each new discovery.

We must recognize that great truths can be misunderstood unless they are carefully probed and examined. The details are to be explored to the fullest. We are to grasp in its entirety *That Christ may dwell in your hearts by faith; that ye being rooted and grounded in love.* This is a tremendous statement, requiring the strength of the Holy Spirit working within us in order for us to grasp its importance and significance. It is a privilege to ponder these words and the thoughts contained behind them and within them.

Two thoughts should be borne in mind. This prayer is offered for those who are believers in Christ and it is offered for all believers, the evangels, the preachers, the teachers, and each member of Christ's body. *And he* (himself) *gave some, apostles; and some, prophets; and some, evangelists; and some, pastors and teachers* [Eph. 4:11]. There is not any one group in the New Testament that has a special position or place of honor.

When considering the great truths of the Bible there is one that oft times may be overlooked or passed by rather rapidly. That is the difference between what Christ does "for" you and what Christ does "in" you. Our earliest Christian experiences relating to Christ are based upon what Christ does "for" us. All of us remember with joy in our hearts the tune, "Jesus Loves Me."

We hear about Jesus coming into the world, performing miracles, teaching and feeding the people, ministering to the needs of many, going to the Cross, shedding His blood, dying for us, atoning for us, and being resurrected for us. All these things and many more are what He has done "for" us.

But we are not to stop there. We are to know Christ "in us." We are to know what He can do "in us" and what wonders He can perform. However, that is where we and many others have trouble. We like Him doing "for" us. We love and enjoy Him doing "for" us. The difficulty comes in allowing, in wanting, in desiring Him to do "in" us. We seem to say that is going too far.

The old mindset gets in the way. We like ourselves and do not cotton to the idea that He should dwell "in" us and bring about changes "in" us. That is going too far. However, we are to progress to the point where we gladly want Him "in" us.

Why? Because it is Christ dwelling within the believer, not just as an influence, not as a memory, or a desire, or His teachings. It is much more than that. It is Christ Himself dwelling in some mystical manner.

> *To whom God would* (willed to) *make known what is the riches of the glory of this mystery among the Gentiles; which is Christ in you, the hope of glory* [Col. 1:27].
>
> *I am crucified with Christ: nevertheless I live; yet not I, but Christ liveth in me: and the life which I now live in the flesh I live by the faith of* (faith in) *the Son of God, who loved me, and gave himself for me* [Gal. 2:20].

Note these verses that say *Christ in you, Christ liveth in me*. These verses describe a mystical relationship and union.

What do we say when someone asks, "What do you mean Christ dwells in you and in me?" They say they do not understand it. Of course, we cannot fully understand. Nobody can. We are told our bodies are holy temples in which the Spirit dwelleth. The Holy Ghost is in heaven and in us. Jesus Christ is in heaven and in us.

Though we may not fully understand this most wonderful truth, pray God that He will grant unto us the faith and joy of hymn writers like Bernard of Clairvaux, who wrote "Jesus the Very Thought of Thee" that beautifully expresses the thoughts of true believers.

> *Jesus, the very thought of thee*
> *With sweetness fills the breast;*
> *O hope of every contrite heart,*
> *O joy of all the meek,*
> *To those who fall, how kind thou art!*
> *How good to those who seek!*
> *But what to those who find?*
> *Ah, this Nor tongue nor pen can show:*
> *The love of Jesus, what it is*
> *None but His loved ones know.*

What beautiful truths are contained in these verses. *"How good to those who seek! . . . None but His loved ones know."* They may not be able to express it as they wish, but they know it. Therefore, we are to grow and mature until we know it.

There is another hymn by the same writer, "O Jesus, King Most Wonderful," that ineffably describes the Lord Jesus.

> *O Jesus, King most wonderful,*
> *Thou conqueror renowned,*
> *Thou sweetness most ineffable*
> *In whom all joys are found!*

> *When once thou visitest the heart*
> *Then truth begins to shine;*
> *Then earthly vanities depart;*
> *Then kindles love divine.*

Charles Wesley describes in a meaningful way the Lord Jesus and those He calls His own in the hymn "Jesus, Lover of My Soul."

> *Thou, O Christ, art all I want;*
> *More than all in thee I find:*
> *Raise the fallen, cheer the faint,*
> *Heal the sick, and lead the blind.*
> *Just and holy is thy name;*
> *I am all unrighteousness;*
> *False and full of sin I am,*
> *Thou art full of truth and grace.*

How does all this become possible to us? What do we have to do? Pray to God the Father through the Lord Jesus Christ, *That he would grant you, according to the riches of his glory, to be strengthened with might by his Spirit in the inner man* [Eph. 3:16].

The Apostle prays that God grant us according to the riches of His glory that we will be strengthened with might by His Spirit. He prays that the Holy Spirit will work in our minds, hearts, and wills. We need to be strengthened so we can comprehend the great truths of Christ, so that we can grasp hold of them and not allow them to elude us.

We are to pray for the Holy Spirit to strengthen the love of Christ within us and to strengthen our wills. We should follow the Apostle's example and pray not only for ourselves, but also for each other.

The more we are strengthened, the more we will want to be strengthened and the more we will want to prepare our hearts and minds for Him. It may seem like an ongoing circle, and in one respect it is, but the circle gets larger and larger and stronger and stronger.

It can be like the mighty oak. As a seedling it is still an oak tree, but as the circles grow it becomes stronger and stronger. The more it is nourished, the stronger it grows, and the circles become larger. This is where faith comes in, *That Christ may dwell in your hearts by faith.* We believe it is possible, we know it can become a reality.

However, this does not mean "taking it by faith," which is more or less persuading yourself He has come. No, it is like the writers of the hymns; they knew it was a fact. They knew He was dwelling within them.

Pray God that we have the strength of mind, heart, and will to grasp hold of Him, that He will dwell in us, and that He will settle down and make His abode within us.

Amen!

11

Preparing the Heart

> *That Christ may dwell in your hearts by faith; that ye, being rooted and grounded in love, . . .* [Eph. 3:17].

This is a profound verse, requiring our positive attention and contemplation. Note the sequence of Paul's prayer:

> *That he would grant you, according to the riches of his glory, to be strengthened with might by His Spirit in the inner man;*
> *That Christ may dwell in your hearts by faith; that ye, being rooted and grounded in love, . . .* [Eph. 3:16–17].

Christ's followers are to know these truths in detail. We are not to gloss over them. They are for our benefit and enrichment. If we were really selfish and thought of ourselves in a positive manner we would lose our hearts, minds, and souls *in Christ*, so we would benefit from the riches available to us. Instead we remain self-centered and narrow, which results in shutting out the blessings God wishes to bestow upon us.

We are to know how *to be strengthened*, how to prepare our hearts, and how to be *rooted and grounded in love*. As Calvin noted, Paul "explains the nature of the strength of the inward man." God placed the fullness of all gifts *in Christ*, so the person who has been strengthened with might by the Spirit and has Christ dwelling in his or her heart can want for nothing.

A person is mistaken who hopes to obtain the Holy Spirit apart from Christ, and they are equally foolish to believe Christ can be received without the Spirit. The two go together. The one cannot be found without the other. "Paul well defines those who are endowed with the spiritual power of God as those in whom Christ dwells," as described by John Calvin.

It is in our hearts where Christ truly dwells. The heart, according to Scripture, is the center of our being. It is not sufficient for Him to be on our tongues, or to bounce around in our brains from time to time or on Sundays only, but to be in our hearts day in and day out.

Paul prays that we may realize the reality of being *in Christ* and that Christ may dwell within us. He wants us to be what we are meant to be. He wants us to experience the intimate and powerful relationship with Christ in our hearts, minds, and wills. He wants us to hunger and thirst after righteousness, but after nothing else.

How does Christ dwell in our hearts? How do we achieve an intimate, personal relationship with Him? The Apostle says, *By faith*. This phrase certainly can be misinterpreted. As previously stated, it does not mean taking it by faith. Yes, it is by faith that we acknowledge Christ suffered for us, died for us, and rose for us. It is also by faith that we receive Him, possess Him, and enjoy Him, and by faith that He operates within us.

Believing in Christ and having fellowship with Him are not exactly the same things. The effect of faith is to have fellowship with Christ. This fellowship is not to be viewed from a distance, but is to be received and embraced so that Christ may dwell in us and that we may be filled with the Holy Spirit.

What does *by faith* mean? Otto Weber says, "Faith is human behavior." God does not "believe," nor does the Holy Spirit "believe." We believe. The New Testament speaks primarily of the faith which man has, not what God has. Who is the person who has faith? It is not the person who is in Adam. It is the person who is a new creature, as the Apostle Paul appropriately stated, *Therefore, if any man be in Christ, he is a new creature* (creation): *old things are passed away; behold, all things are become new* [2 Cor. 5:17]. They become new in us. The believing person is a new creation. This term is not to be contrasted with the "old creation," but with the perversion and deterioration of creatureliness.

It is to be understood with respect to our salvation as established by Christ Jesus. God does what man by himself cannot do. Paul was well aware of the inward man. He expressed his thoughts to the Romans, Corinthians, and Ephesians, saying,

> *O wretched man that I am! Who shall deliver me from the body of this death* (this body of death) [Rom. 7:24]?

> *For which cause we faint not* (do not lose heart), *but though our outward man perish* (is perishing), *yet the inward man is renewed day by day* [2 Cor. 4:16].

> *That he would grant you, according to the riches of his glory, to be strengthened with might by his Spirit in the inner man* [Eph. 3:16].

All of this accords with the inward man, or the inmost self.

The "possibility" and "reality" of faith are found in God's faithfulness. God has established His covenant. He has abided by it through the ages, and He will continue to do so. This is how faith lives on. God's dowry is His faithfulness, which Paul emphasizes in these two meaningful questions: *For what if some did not believe? shall their* (our) *unbelief make the faith* (faithfulness) *of God without effect* [Rom. 3:3]?

God is faithful in calling us, in preserving us, and in forgiving us. God keeps nothing for Himself. God's faithfulness consists of giving Himself to us, yet remaining Himself while He is doing it. The response to God's faithfulness is the truth, confidence, and commitment of the creature, the individual, to God. This is what God desires, and it is the object of His faithfulness.

How does God do this? He discloses Himself to us in Christ Jesus. This allows us to receive Him in person and to respond to Him in person.

What does God's faithfulness do? It calls forth our faith, it strengthens our faith, and it allows us to grasp our faith, as noted in the following: *Not as though I had already attained, either were already perfect: but I follow after, if that I may apprehend that for which also I am apprehended of Christ Jesus* [Phil. 3:12].

It is important to consider a certain truth at this time. Unfortunately, people seem to have one of two primary ideas: Either they are waiting for their faith to happen through some memorable event, or they complain that nothing has happened to them.

People would very much like to be bowled over by God. When they do not have an experience they want, or that they would mandate God to perform, then they seal themselves off and embark upon their own course.

On the other hand, there are people who seek out subjective experiences. They search for "faith healing," or "personality cults," or something else that will overwhelm them, which they can say is the Holy Spirit according to their emotional ideas or feelings.

Certain points need to be asserted in this regard.

First, faith according to the Bible does not consist of a person being set aside, but of the individual being involved to the utmost.

Second, God's faithfulness is not some power that functions with the impact of the force of nature, like a hurricane or tidal wave, but in the person of Jesus Christ.

Third, there is only one way by which God's faithfulness enters into our presence and dwells in our hearts. It comes from the outside and becomes the object of our trust.

Fourth, faith is dealing with God as He discloses Himself through Jesus Christ.

Fifth, faith does not rest on ignorance, but on knowledge. It is not the authority of the church nor the power of emotional involvement that establishes and preserves faith. The knowledge obtained is the self-disclosure of God through the Lord Jesus Christ.

What additional thoughts are contained in the phrase *by faith*? It is not a passive state. The eleventh chapter of Hebrews reveals that faith is active. It was active in the lives of Abel, Enoch, Noah, Abraham, Sarah, Isaac, Jacob, Joseph, Moses, Gideon, Barak, Samson, Jepthah, David, Samuel, and the prophets. *These all died in faith, not having received the promises, but having seen them afar off, and were persuaded* (assured) *of them, and embraced them, and confessed that they were strangers and pilgrims on the earth* [Heb. 11:13]. This definition of faith allows us to discover the meaning of the words, *That Christ may dwell in your hearts by faith*. We are to recognize this teaching, see it and grasp it, but we are not to consider it superficially.

The men noted in Hebrews, the eleventh chapter, were living their lives in the world; they were doing their jobs or tasks. While they were, a message came from God to do something different. They believed it was from God, and they did it, even when they were ridiculed or asked to do something that seemed unthinkable or impossible.

Hopefully, we see from this illustration that the people *in Christ* see the possibility of doing something. They see it, others do not. Unless we see the reality of something, we shall never experience it.

A second factor is that these people were persuaded. They did not reject, or pooh-pooh, or belittle the task to which they were called. They did not offer countless excuses or completely turn away from the project. They did not say that their position, or job, or peculiar circumstances would prevent them from doing what was requested or commanded.

The author of the letter to the Hebrews notes that the people identified in this magnificent chapter *embraced* the promises in faith. It does not say that they embraced them easily, readily, quickly, or glibly. This verse says, *having seen them afar off, and were persuaded* (assured) *of them*. They were persuaded, even though they had questions, trials, and tests; they had faith, and they embraced the promises.

Gerhard Tersteegen's hymn, "Thou Hidden Love of God," may help us to understand this fact.

> *Thou hidden love of God, whose height,*
> *Whose depth unfathomed, no man knows,*
> *I see from afar thy beauteous light,*
> *Inwardly I sigh for thy repose;*
> *My heart is pained, nor can it be*
> *At rest until it finds rest in thee.*
> *Tis mercy all, that thou has brought*
> *My mind to seek her peace in thee;*
> *Yet, while I seek but find thee not,*
> *No peace my wandering soul shall see;*
> *O when shall all my wanderings end,*
> *And all my steps to thee-ward tend.*

Apparently, this writer struggled. He sought it and did not want it to elude him. He wanted to embrace it.

Next, the author of Hebrews states, *and confessed that they were strangers and pilgrims on the earth*. It was at this point that they began to act. There is a time in our lives *in Christ* when we must begin to live the promises we have embraced. Abraham embraced the promises *when he was called to go out into a place which he should after receive for an inheritance, obeyed; and he went out, not knowing whither he went* (where he was going) [Heb. 11:8]. Abraham confessed, embraced, and acted. His life became a testimony to the reality of God.

What practical things can we do for Christ to dwell in our hearts by faith?

The first thing, which sounds rather simple, is to keep this reality constantly in our hearts. However, it requires effort, reading your Bible, meditating on Scripture, singing or listening to hymns, reading biographies or books, praying, and establishing priorities.

Second, we are to constantly remind ourselves that our relationship with Jesus Christ is personal. Yes, we may believe on Him, recognize what He has done for us, and accept certain principles of the Christian faith. But the question is, do we have a personal relationship with Him, and do we have the strength to grab hold and have Him settle down within us?

Ernest Logan, an Irishman who was an associate minister at the First Presbyterian Church in Pittsburgh in the 1960s and 1970s, would ask individuals joining the church about their Christian experiences. He would listen patiently as they talked about their lives as children and growing up in a fine home, about the various jobs or functions they had performed in the churches to which they had belonged, or about the boards on which they may have served. Then he would say, "Aye, that is all very well and good, but would ye mind telling me about your relationship to the Lord Jesus Christ?" Usually, this caused consternation and long pauses before eliciting a response. Ernest had a way of cutting to the heart of the matter. It is our relationship with Christ that is important, nothing more, nothing less, nothing else.

Third, we must realize that certain things are incompatible with having a personal relationship with Christ. Paul speaks directly to the Corinthians with boldness,

- pointing out their hard-heartedness, yet softening his rebuke by calling them children;
- stating that they are not restricted by his message and Christ Jesus, but by their own affections;
- stating that they should enlarge their hearts, so that they can repay the affection of such a kind Father;
- stating that they are not to be *unequally yoked together with unbelievers: for what fellowship* (in common) *hath righteousness with unrighteousness* (lawlessness) [2 Cor. 6:14];
- asking, *what concord* (accord) *hath Christ with Belial* [2 Cor. 6:15];

- saying it is absurd and unnatural to connect themselves to anything so opposed to their faith in Christ as idolatry;
- stating that idolatry is a sin and that *Ye are the temple of the living God* [2 Cor. 6:16];
- reminding them that, *God hath said, I WILL DWELL IN THEM, AND WALK IN THEM; AND I WILL BE THEIR GOD, AND THEY SHALL BE MY PEOPLE* [2 Cor. 6:16];
- declaring that God also said since I am your God *COME OUT FROM AMONG THEM, AND BE YE SEPARATE, . . . AND TOUCH NOT THE UNCLEAN THING; AND I WILL RECEIVE YOU, AND WILL BE A FATHER UNTO YOU, AND YE SHALL BE MY SONS AND DAUGHTERS* [2 Cor. 6:17–18];
- urging them, as only he could, *Having therefore these promises, dearly beloved, let us cleanse ourselves from all filthiness of the flesh and the spirit, perfecting holiness in the fear of God* [2 Cor. 7:1].

Paul admonishes them, enlightens them, reminds them, and urges them to action. May we hearken to his words.

Since we have been redeemed by God's grace, we are to keep ourselves undefiled from any impurity. If we do not, then we pollute the sanctuary of God. Therefore, we are to avoid all participation with uncleanness. God's promise to be a Father should motivate us to desire holiness and purity. We are to remember Paul's admonition to *cleanse ourselves from all filthiness of the flesh and spirit, perfecting holiness in the fear of God*.

Fourth, if we do these things there is something else to consider of which we should be aware: The Apostle John says, *Love not the world, neither the things that are in the world. If any man love the world, the love of the Father is not in him* [1 John 2:15].

You cannot have the love of the Father and the world at the same time. However, even when you remove the world from your heart, mind, and will, there is something else to address. What is it? Self! Christ and sinful self cannot dwell in the heart at the same time. We should be aware of this. If Christ is to dwell within us and occupy our hearts, then self must abdicate.

There is a wonderful poem titled "None of Self and All of Thee," by the Frenchman Theodore Monod, that expresses this thought in a very meaningful way.

> *Oh, the bitter shame and sorrow*
> *That a time could ever be*
> *When I let the Saviour's pity*
> *Plead in vain, and proudly answered,*
> *All of self and none of Thee.*
>
> *Yet He found me; I beheld Him*
> *Bleeding on the accursed tree;*
> *Heard Him pray, "Forgive them, Father";*
> *And my wistful heart said faintly,*
> *Some of self and some of Thee.*
>
> *Day by day, His tender mercy,*
> *Healing, helping, full and free,*
> *Sweet and strong, and, oh, so patient,*
> *Brought me lower, while I whispered,*
> *Less of self and more of Thee.*
>
> *Higher than the highest heavens,*
> *Deeper than the deepest sea,*
> *Lord, Thy love at last has conquered;*
> *Grant me now my soul's desire,*
> *None of self and all of Thee.*

Certainly we should be able to relate to some of these beautiful thoughts and confessions, and someday, hopefully, to all of them.

Fifth, we must realize our utter dependence. Therefore, we must spend time in prayer. We are to talk with Christ and ask Him to settle down in our hearts, to cleanse us, purify us, and strengthen us. Prayer is essential for Christ to dwell in our hearts by faith.

Sixth, we must persevere. The going will be tough. There will be discouragements and disappointments. Thoughts will enter our minds, and we will wonder, where did that come from?

But we must persevere. Why? Because as Jesus promises, *All that the father giveth me shall come to me; and him that cometh to me I will in no wise* (certainly not) *cast out* [John 6:37]. We should remember these words, especially when things look bleak or are not going as we wish. God answers our prayers. However, we are to persevere in offering them.

Seventh, we are to be obedient. There is knowledge, assent, trust, and obedience in faith. Rudolph Bultman said of Paul, "In him faith is understood as primarily obedience." This is seen after Paul's conversion and spending three years in the wilderness with the Lord Jesus. It is evidenced by his obedience, citing passages and interpreting them, surrendering his will to the Lord Jesus, and proceeding in a different direction.

What happens to an individual? He or she is converted and as a result belongs to another ruler. This results in *Casting down imaginations* (arguments), *and every high thing that exalteth itself against the knowledge of God, and bringing into captivity every thought to the obedience of Christ* [2 Cor. 10:5]. May we take every thought captive and obey Christ.

Faith consists of the fact that we accept God as our God and Jesus Christ as our Lord. We obey, we emerge, we develop, we proceed. We are no longer our own master, but we belong to the Master. Obedience belongs solely to faith.

May we remember the beautiful, truthful thoughts contained in Monod's poem as we proceed from "All of self and none of Thee" to "None of self and all of Thee."

Amen!

12

Love and Knowledge

> *That Christ may dwell in your hearts by faith; that ye, being rooted and grounded in love,* . . . [Eph. 3:17].

Paul proceeds from Christ dwelling in our hearts by faith to the next truth *that ye, being rooted and grounded in love*. What does he mean by this phrase? What does he want the Ephesian followers to grasp? *That ye, being rooted and grounded in love, May be able to comprehend* (understand). The Apostle's concern for these people is that they may know the Lord Jesus Christ. He prays that He may dwell in their hearts.

There is one significant point in the New Testament about the love of God that is also true of the Old Testament. That is, the love of God for people can be summed up in two words: Jesus Christ. The New Testament stresses first and foremost that we are to seek a personal relationship with the Lord Jesus. We are not to seek blessings, holiness, sanctification, or anything else first, but only the Lord Jesus Christ.

All our blessings are a result of knowing Him, having fellowship with Him, having communion with Him, and loving Him because He first loved us. We should desire and pray for not only a deeper and greater knowledge of Him, but for the love of Him. When our love grows stronger, so will our spiritual life and our faith.

The Apostle prays that Christ will dwell in our hearts so that we will be *rooted and grounded in love*. Please note the order in which these items are discussed, the sequence of the thoughts and the prayer.

What is the first result of Christ dwelling in our hearts? We become *rooted and grounded in love*. Paul does not pray that we become *rooted and grounded* in God's love. That comes later. We do not have any real love apart from His love. Why? We love Him because He first loved us.

How can we really believe that Christ came, went to the Cross, shed His blood, endured the pain and shame, and died for us without having a deep feeling of true love towards Him? The Apostle wants us to focus attention on our love towards Christ, more so than His love toward us. Remember, we have discussed what Christ has done for us and what Christ can do in us. The Apostle wants us to devote our thoughts to our love for God and Christ, our love towards our fellow members in the community of believers, and our love towards everything pertaining to the truth revealed in the person and work of Jesus Christ.

The Apostle uses two illustrations to present a meaningful picture: a tree and a building. They have similarities and dissimilarities. The similarities are that they both present a picture of permanence, depth, firmness, strength, and the ability to stand the test of time.

When considering the word *rooted*, think of a large oak with its roots reaching deep into the earth, taking a firm hold, and receiving nourishment from the available nutrients, and providing protection, food, comfort, and a home to various animals, birds, and people.

The word *grounded* causes us to think of great buildings constructed on strong foundations. Both the tree and the building are impressive because they are solid and will stand the test of time against various tests, trials, and tribulations.

However, there are dissimilarities. The tree presents signs of life, vitality, energy, growth, and renewal. A building suggests strength that can withstand stresses and strains and other influences brought to bear upon it. When thinking of *rooted and grounded*, our thoughts race to the closing verses of the Sermon on the Mount.

> *Therefore whosoever heareth these sayings of mine, and doeth them, I will liken him unto a wise man, which built his house upon a (the) rock:*
> *And the rain descended, and floods came, and the winds blew, and beat upon that house; and it fell not: for it was founded upon a (the) rock.*
> *And everyone that heareth these sayings of mine, and doeth them not, shall be likened unto a foolish man, which built his house upon the sand:*
> *And the rain descended, and the floods came, and the winds blew, and beat upon that house; and it fell: and great was the fall of it* [Matt. 7:24–27].

These beautiful verses enable us to realize that unless the Gospel is firmly embedded in our hearts it is like a high wall that is erected without any support. Faith comes when it has deep roots in the heart and builds on a base of serious and enduring commitments, which yield less and less to temptations. In a similar way, when Christ dwells in your heart by faith *ye will be rooted and grounded in love.* Note what comes first.

The first picture is one of being *rooted* in love. The great oak tree stands majestically with its roots spreading out and penetrating deep into the soil. Its roots are actually trees in themselves. They have great strength and reach into the earth. It is difficult for them to be blown over, and if perchance they are they raise a tremendous amount of dirt. This is the description of the followers of Christ, whose roots go deep into the Master and have the strength to grab hold of Him. Further, the tree cannot be shaken since the roots are deep and strong. And that is to be the condition of the followers in the Way.

This picture generates the idea that love is the soil in which our life *in Christ* dwells and grows. The nourishment that strengthens us and enables us to grow comes from the soil and its moisture. Love builds up our life *in Christ* and makes that life like the life of Christ Himself. We are to look to Him when we are tempted to make comparisons, and to realize we are to become more and more like Him. We are not to compare ourselves with other people for better or worse, but only with Christ. And, that makes a difference.

The Apostle prays for those who have accepted Christ, who believe and have been sealed with the Spirit. He prays that they will advance from their initial experiences and proceed to full maturity *in Christ.*

Finally, we are to realize that the only way to become *rooted* in love is to become like Him. The real strength of the life *in Christ* is love. There is nothing stronger than true love, the love *in Christ*. It is the most powerful influence in the world.

What does Scripture say about true love *in Christ*? The New Testament teaches that it is love *in Christ*, not knowledge, that makes us strong followers in the Way. Paul says, *Knowledge puffeth up, but charity* (love) *edifieth* (builds up) [1 Cor. 8:1]. Remember, Paul said this. Paul is the one who encourages knowledge, who wants us to know more and more, who wants us to grow in knowledge. Yet he is the one who says *Knowledge puffeth up.*

The renowned John Calvin's wisdom provides additional light regarding Paul's statement that *Knowledge puffeth up, but charity* (love) *edifieth* (builds up). Calvin says that Paul "shows from the effects just how stupid it is to boast about knowledge, when love is absent. He could have expressed himself like this: 'What is the use of knowledge, when all it does is to make us swollen-headed, and superior, whereas it is of the very essence of love to edify?' This passage, which otherwise would be secure because of its conciseness, can easily be understood in this way: 'Anything which lacks even a suggestion of love, is worthless in God's sight, is in fact displeasing to Him—how much more so anything that openly joins battle with love? But this knowledge, about which you Corinthians boast, is definitely in the opposite camp to love, for it fills men with arrogance, and makes them look contemptuously on their brothers. Love, on the other hand, moves us to concern for our brothers, and encourages us to look to their upbuilding. No wonder I would say, accursed be that knowledge which produces arrogant men, and is untouched by a concern for other people's welfare!'

"Again, he (Paul) did not mean that learning, by its nature breeds arrogance. He simply wanted to show the effect that knowledge has on men, when fear of God and love of the brethren are lacking. For unbelievers do take advantage of all the gifts of God in order to put themselves on a pedestal. Thus riches, honours, official positions, high birth, good looks and similar things go to people's heads; for they are carried away by a misplaced confidence in them, and become as arrogant as can be. Of course it its not always so, for we come across many people who are wealthy, good-looking, weighed down with honours, holding official positions, of noble birth, who remain humble people all the same, and have not a scrap of pride about them.

"Therefore it must be accepted that knowledge is good in itself, but because religion is the one and only basis for it, it becomes a futile, fading thing, so far as unbelievers are concerned, for love is its essential seasoning, and without that, it is ineffectual. Indeed where there is no sign of that serious knowledge of God, which humbles us and teaches us to be concerned about our brothers, what you discover is something which is imagined to be knowledge, rather than knowledge itself, and that in those who are looked upon as the most learned. But knowledge must no more be blamed for this, than a sword for falling into the hands of a madman. . . . But those very people who decry them like this are so vociferous in their pride, that they are living exemplars of the old proverb: 'Nothing is so arrogant as ignorance.'"

Paul's first letter to the Corinthians diligently considers both love and knowledge. When the Apostle wrote to the Corinthians he knew they were beset by different problems. He realized they were putting knowledge in place of love. They were emphasizing knowledge and making it the supreme thing in the life of the community of believers. The followers in Corinth were a gifted group. However, they went astray on an important point. They had forgotten love and placed a heavy emphasis on knowledge. Love is the foundation upon which everything else is built. This is an important point; do not dilute it.

Knowledge is important, and it is essential, because without it we cannot grow in our spiritual life, our life *in Christ*. When we are *in Christ*, knowledge is never purely intellectual. Why? Because it is knowledge of a person. A marriage can never be purely intellectual if it is to be enduring. The relationship between parent and child can never be purely intellectual.

The purpose of the doctrine we have been studying and the knowledge we have been acquiring is one and the same. It is to bring us to the foot of the Cross. It is to bring us to our Lord and Saviour Jesus Christ. It is to bring us into a personal relationship with the Son of God. Everything is directed to kindling a love that cannot be extinguished, one that will grow and grow and grow because it is rooted in a soil providing the necessary nutrients.

The primacy of this love is emphasized again and again. Why? Because it has been a pitfall to many people during the last twenty centuries. What approaches are taken by different people?

Some do not concern themselves with knowledge at all. They want to ignore it. Others think knowledge is most important and that nothing else matters. So they pursue it to the detriment of everything else. Consequently, Satan turns their thoughts to purely intellectual items.

What is the result? Their minds become jammed with knowledge, facts, and doctrine, but their hearts become hard and cold.

True knowledge about faith in Christ is an intimate knowledge of the Person to whom all Scripture leads, Jesus Christ. Since it is knowledge of this Person, it leads us to love Him because He Himself is love.

In reality, to know God and to know Christ leads to love. If the knowledge we obtain does not produce a greater love in our lives, then we had better examine ourselves.

Knowledge without love does not produce pleasurable results. It makes one "high-minded." Paul provides the best definition and description of love. Note what he says in these verses,

> . . . *have not charity* (love), *I am nothing.*
> . . . *And have not charity* (love), *it profiteth me nothing,*
> *Charity* (love) *suffereth long, and is kind; charity* (love) *envieth not; charity* (love) *vaunteth not* (does not brag on) *itself, is not puffed up* (arrogant),
> *Doth not behave itself unseemly* (rudely), *seeketh not her own, is not easily provoked, thinketh no evil* (keeps no account of evil);
> *Rejoiceth not in iniquity, but rejoiceth in the truth;*
> *Beareth all things, believeth all things, hopeth all things, endureth all things.*
> *Charity never faileth*
> [Selections from 1 Cor. 13:2–8].

Consider what follows these truths:

> *But when that which is perfect* (complete) *is come, then that which is in part shall be done away.*
> *When I was a child, I spake as a child, I understood as a child, I thought as a child: but when I became a man, I put away childish things.*
> *For now we see through a glass, darkly* (dimly); *but then face to face: now I know in part; but then shall I know even as also I am known.*
> *And now abideth faith, hope, charity* (love), *these three; but the greatest of these is charity* (love) [1 Cor. 13:10–13].

What does Scripture have to say about knowledge and love? Do you remember the Scripture at the beginning of this exposition from the Sermon on the Mount? The knowledge contained in these verses is for one purpose: to lead us to love. And, in turn, to change our outlook, our thoughts, and our priorities.

> *Ye have heard that it hath been said, AN EYE FOR AN EYE, AND A TOOTH FOR A TOOTH:*
> *But I say unto you, That ye resist not evil* (an evil person): *but whosoever shall smite* (slap) *thee on thy right cheek, turn to him the other also.*

> *And if any man will sue thee at the law, and take away thy coat (tunic), let him have thy cloak also.*
>
> *And whosoever shall compel thee to go a mile, go with him twain (two).*
>
> *Give to him that asketh thee, and from him that would borrow of thee turn not thou away.*
>
> *Ye have heard that it hath been said, THOU SHALT LOVE THY NEIGHBOR, and hate thine enemy.*
>
> *But I say unto you, Love your enemies, bless them that curse you, do good to them that hate you, and pray for them which despitefully (spitefully) use you, and persecute you;*
>
> *That ye may be the children (sons) of your Father which is in heaven: for he maketh his sun to rise on the evil and on the good, and sendeth rain on the just and on the unjust.*
>
> *For if ye love them which love you, what reward have ye? do not even the publicans (tax collectors) the same?*
>
> *And if ye salute (greet) your brethren only, what do ye more than others? do not even the publicans* (tax collectors) *so* [Matt. 5:38–47]*?*

Then comes Jesus' powerful command: *Be ye therefore perfect, even as your Father which is in heaven is perfect* [Matt. 5:48].

In these ten verses our Lord Jesus Christ uses words, phrases, and thoughts with which the listeners were familiar. It is amazing how current the Gospel of Christ is because it is directed to the heart of man. Christ makes all these points to show that God's love is perfect and that we are to be perfect.

Do you see what Christ does? He provides the map, the itinerary, and the knowledge. Why? For only one reason, to lead His followers to the love of God, which is made perfect *in Christ*.

We are to think about these truths. Even more important, we are to put them into practice so that our love of Christ will grow. In turn, our love for those with whom we come into contact and with whom we disagree will grow.

Remember what was said previously. We love to hear and think about what Christ has done for us, but we do not have the same enthusiasm for what the Lord Jesus can do *in us*. We need the knowledge, we need to practice what Christ taught, but above all we need the love of Christ *in us*.

What does the Apostle Paul say about faith and love? *For in Jesus Christ neither circumcision availeth any thing, nor uncircumcision; but faith which worketh by love* [Gal. 5:6].

The Apostle rarely mentions faith without tying in love. Faith and love go together. Paul prays *that Christ may dwell in your hearts by faith;* then he immediately continues his prayer by petitioning *that ye, being rooted and grounded in love.* Why does Paul tie faith and love together? Because faith works by love, faith is energized by love, and a life of faith is active because of love.

Have you ever thought that love energizes you and it energizes others? Think of what a loving mother does for her family and her children. Love energizes her, which in turn energizes the family.

We are familiar with the story of Jacob and Rachel. What impact did love have on Jacob? *And Jacob served seven years for Rachel; and they seemed unto him but a few days, for* (because of) *the love he had to* (for) *her* [Gen. 29:20]. It was the power of his love that made the time seem so short. His love for Rachel did not count the time or the cost.

What about the followers in the Way, the disciples, the members of the community of believers, the ministers, evangels, teachers, laity, and all the others during the past two thousand years? What has motivated them? Why do they call themselves Christians? Why do they say they are *in Christ*? Why do they partake of the elements in the Lord's Supper? Why do they believe Christ died for their sins?

The answer to all these questions is one and the same. *For God so loved the world, that He gave His only begotten Son* [John 3:16]. Why did God do this? Not just for man or mankind, but for you and me individually. Because of His love, Matthew, Mark, and Luke each relate how Jesus had compassion for the multitudes, for the disciples, and for us.

In each of these situations the word used for *compassion* in Greek means, "to have the bowels yearning," to have everything in you yearning for the other person, to be wrenching, to be torn apart. With Christ in us, our love for those in need or requiring great love is to be like that of Christ toward those in need.

When considering these thoughts, one should ask other questions about love. What should be the motive for holy living? Love. Because endeavoring to live the holy life pleases God, whereas sin displeases Him. The true motive for thinking, practicing, and living as Christ would have us to do is that it grieves God and offends Him when we do not try to live the holy life.

Our desire should be to please God, not simply to obey different commandments, but to give joy to God and the Lord Jesus Christ. The love of Christ should be our motive. When it is, it has an impact on what we do, why we do it, and how we do it. How did this love apply to Paul? The Apostle traveled many, many miles and endured hardships, cruelties, and indignities. Why did he do as he did? The reason, *For the love of Christ constraineth us* [2 Cor. 5:14]. This means that it controls and compels us.

Calvin amplifies upon why Christ's love should control and compel us saying, "the measureless love of Christ towards us, of which He gave us evidence by His death. The knowledge of this love should constrain our feelings so that we cannot but love Him in return. The metaphor in the word *constrain* brings out the point that everyone who truly considers and ponders the wonderful love that Christ has shown us in His death, cannot but be bound to Him by the tightest chain so as to devote Himself to His service."

Paul states the need for love emphatically and succinctly by describing its characteristics in 1 Corinthians, chapter 13. When examining that chapter, you realize what a shattering and penetrating statement it is, as well as the eternal truths contained in those verses. This should impact our thinking, our motives, and our daily living. The life *in Christ* is to be Christ-like, and everything *in Christ* has its source in true love.

This is not the teaching of Paul only. Think of the poor widow that Christ observed entering the treasury. He saw her as she

> . . . *threw in two mites, which make a farthing* (one-fourth of a penny).
> *And he called unto him his disciples, and saith . . . Verily, I say unto you, that this poor widow hath cast more in, than all they which have cast into the treasury:*
> *For all they did cast in of their abundance* (surplus); *but she of her want* (out of her poverty) *did cast in all that she had, even all her living* (whole livelihood) [Mark 12:42–44].

While living in the Pittsburgh area, we attended the First Presbyterian Church, which is located in the heart of the city. It was my privilege to usher in the balcony, where an elderly gentleman sat in the same pew every Sunday. He lived at the top of Mt. Washington, which is across the

Monongahela River from the city. The distance is approximately three to four miles. This gentleman walked that distance twice every Sunday in all types of weather, even in the coldest winter weather months. One Sunday I said to him "Why don't you take the street car?" He responded: "Bob, I do not have very much money. By walking I can take the street car money and put it in the offering plate." He cast his mite in out of his want, with a joyful heart.

Think of the woman who washed Jesus' feet with her tears, wiped them with the hair of her head, and anointed them with ointment. What did Jesus say of her? *Wherefore I say unto thee, Her sins, which are many, are forgiven; for she loved much: but to whom little is forgiven, the same loveth little* [Luke 7:47].

The person who is *in Christ* is not one who performs a task or duty or chore. It is the person who is *rooted in love*. It is the person who is constrained, controlled, and compelled by the love of Christ.

Calvin states it so clearly, "The word constrain points out that everyone who truly considers and ponders the wonderful love that Christ has shown us in His death, cannot but be bound to Him by the tightest chain so as to devote Himself to His service." It is the person who has Christ dwelling in his heart by faith. It is the person having a personal relationship with Christ as friend, Saviour, and the Son of God. Pray God that He will bless us with His deep and abiding love.

The love of Christ and our love to Him are wondrously stated in that old hymn, "The Old Rugged Cross," by George Bennard that was removed from our hymnals. What a travesty that was! It may have been removed from the hymnals, but it cannot be removed from our hearts and minds. It expresses the truth of Calvary's Hill, which should be proclaimed, and proclaimed forevermore. It goes like this:

> *On a hill far away stood an old rugged cross,*
> *The emblem of suffering and shame,*
> *And I love that old cross where the dearest and best*
> *For a world of lost sinners was slain.*
>
> Refrain
>
> *So I'll cherish the old rugged cross*
> *Till my trophies at last I lay down;*
> *I will cling to the old rugged cross and*
> *exchange it some day for a crown.*

Oh, that old rugged cross so despised by the world,
Has a wondrous attraction for me;
For the dear lamb of God left
His glory above to bear it on dark Calvary.

Refrain

In the old rugged cross,
stained with blood so divine,
A wondrous beauty, I see,
For t'was on that old cross
Jesus suffered and died, to pardon and sanctify me.

Refrain

To the old rugged cross I will ever be true,
Its shame and reproach gladly bear;
Then He'll call me someday to my home far way,
Where His glory forever I'll share.

Refrain

Amen!

13

Life's Foundation

> *That Christ may dwell in your hearts by faith; that ye, being rooted and grounded in love, . . .* [Eph. 3:17].

Paul prays that we might be grounded in love. This precedes his petition that we may be able to comprehend. Once again, Paul, under the influence of the Holy Spirit, proceeds in a natural, logical progression. We must be rooted and grounded in love, if we are to comprehend.

What does this word *love*, or the Greek word *agape* actually mean when used in the New Testament?

It describes God's attitude toward His Son: *that the love wherewith thou* (God) *hast loved me may be in them, and I in them* [John 17:26]. It describes His attitude toward the human race: *For God so loved the world, that he gave his only begotten Son, that whosoever believeth in him should not perish, but have everlasting life* [John 3:16]. And it describes His attitude toward those believing in the Lord Jesus Christ. *He that hath my commandments, and keepeth them, he it is that loveth me: and he that loveth me shall be loved of my Father* [John 14:21].

Love conveys God's will to His children and their attitude toward one another, *For the Father himself loveth you, because ye have loved me, and have believed that I came out from God* [John 16:27]. It also conveys His will regarding their attitude toward all men: *And the Lord make you to increase and abound in love one toward another, and toward all men, even as we do toward you* [1 Thess. 3:12].

Love expresses the essential nature of God; *He that loveth not knoweth not God; for God is love* [1 John 4:8]. And *love* is seen in the gift of His son: *God sent his only begotten Son into the world, that we might live through him. Herein is love, not that we loved God, but that he loved us, and sent his Son to be the propitiation for our sins* [1 John 4:9–10].

It is not a love of complacency or affection, and it certainly does not result because of any excellency or merit in the objects upon whom God bestows His love.

God's gift of His Son was an exercise of divine will and was made for one reason only, to express His love toward us. Love has its perfect expression among people in the person of the Lord Jesus Christ. It is beautifully expressed by Paul in his Letter to the Ephesians: *And to know the love of Christ, which passeth knowledge, that ye might be filled with all the fullness of God* [Eph. 3:19]. Further, the love of those who are *in Christ* is the fruit of the Spirit being in them, as stated in *But the fruit of the Spirit is love* [Gal. 5:22].

What is true regarding the love of those who are *in Christ*? God is the primary object of their love, and they express their love by implicitly obeying God's commandments, as proclaimed by the Lord Jesus when he said, *If ye love me, keep my commandments* [John 14:15].

The love of those *in Christ*, whether exercised toward the brethren or people in general, is not an impulse from emotional feelings, nor is it generated from natural inclinations, nor is it directed only toward those for whom there is some affinity.

Paul amplifies on this in his letter to the Romans, saying,

> *Owe no man anything, but to love one another: for he that loveth another hath fulfilled the law.*
> *For this, THOU SHALT NOT COMMIT ADULTERY, THOU SHALT NOT KILL (MURDER), THOU SHALT NOT STEAL, THOU SHALT NOT BEAR FALSE WITNESS, THOU SHALT NOT COVET; and if there be any other commandment, it is briefly comprehended (summed up) in this saying, namely, THOU SHALT LOVE THY NEIGHBOR AS THYSELF.*
> *Love worketh no ill* (does no harm) *to his neighbor: therefore love is the fulfilling of the law* [Rom. 13:8–10].

Shortly thereafter Paul adds emphasis to his words, saying, *Let every one of us please his neighbor for his good to edification* (being built up) [Rom. 15:2]. Paul also says to the Galatians, *let us do good to all men, especially to them who are of the household of faith* [Gal. 6:10].

God's love (*agape*) expresses the deep, constant love and interest of a perfect God toward entirely unworthy individuals and produces a reverential love in them toward God and a practical love toward one's neighbors. *Agape* love seeks the welfare of all. The Apostle Paul's fundamental proposition is that our lives must be based upon the love of Christ and must draw its strength, power, and nutrients from that love.

What does the Apostle mean by being *grounded in love*? A foundation must be laid upon which to build. It must correspond to the height and weight of the structure, its contents, the potential tests and trials, plus the wear and tear it must withstand. The Apostle says in the third chapter of Ephesians, do not rush your foundation, spend time on it, examine the details, and make sure it will be stronger than necessary to withstand the tests, trials, and temptations of life.

What does our Lord Jesus Christ say? In Luke, He says, *He is like a man which built a house, and digged deep, and laid the foundation on a rock* [Luke 6:48]. In Matthew, our Lord says, *Whosoever heareth these sayings of mine, and doeth them, I will liken him unto a wise man, which built his house upon a* (the) *rock* [Matt. 7:24]. Note this about the man who built upon a rock: He was wise, and he digged deep. And what about the person who built upon the sand? He was foolish, he was without a foundation, he was not interested, and he did not want to be bothered.

The Apostle emphasizes these truths, and in this he is strongly supported by our Lord. There are no shortcuts to the life in the Spirit. It takes time. The Apostle prays that the followers will be filled with the fullness of God because he knows that this cannot happen suddenly or without preparation, but that we must be strengthened, we must dig deep, and we must lay a solid foundation. It is not quick and easy, as some would have us believe.

If we do not take the time to prepare, to be strengthened, to dig deep, and to pour the foundation then we will not know the higher experiences of the life *in Christ*, nor will we know what He can do in us.

It is appropriate to review the words and message of that meaningful hymn "Take Time to be Holy," by William D. Longstaff.

> *Take time to be holy, Speak oft with thy Lord;*
> *Abide in Him always, And feed on His Word.*
> *Make friends of God's children; Help those who are weak;*
> *Forgetting in nothing His blessing to seek.*
>
> *Take time to be holy, The world rushes on;*
> *Much time spend in secret With Jesus alone;*
> *By looking to Jesus, Like Him thou shalt be,*
> *Thy friends, in thy conduct His likeness shall see.*

Take time to be holy, Let Him be thy Guide,
And run not before Him, Whatever betide;
In joy or in sorrow, Still follow thy Lord,
And, looking to Jesus, Still trust in His word.

Take time to be holy, Be calm in thy soul;
Each thought and each motive Beneath His control;
Thus led by His Spirit To fountains of love:
Thou soon shalt be fitted For service above.

What does this foundation mean? What does it contain? First, all the relationships of the life *in Christ* must be based upon love, *agape* love. This is true of the relationship to God and with God. We shall not know the love of God unless our relationship to Him is one of love.

How do we relate to Him? What is our attitude toward Him? The Bible exhorts us to believe in God and to love Him. It calls for a personal relationship with Him, because God is personal, and He desires an intimate relationship.

God is a person; therefore, our relationship to Him through Christ is to be one of love. We are to be clear about loving God, and that love should govern our thinking about Him and how we relate to Him. Further, our attitude toward God is not to be one of fear or dread. *There is no fear in love; but perfect love casteth out fear* [1 John 4:18].

It is vital to take time to discuss and to learn about these matters. It is important to pray to God each day. However, more important than the content of our prayers is our attitude toward God when offering our prayers. Sometimes merely bowing our heads, staying in His presence, and saying nothing is more indicative of a right relationship to God than saying many words or expressing idle thoughts. Contemplating, adoring, and worshipping Him can be the highest expression of our love to God.

The Apostle prays that the lives of the Ephesians will be based upon this foundation. He does not want them to take it for granted. Paul realized that we come to love God as we should when we know Him, know the truth about Him, and know what He has done for us in His Son, Jesus Christ.

Second, we are *not* to stop with just loving God. Scripture says we are to love one another, especially the brethren. This is emphasized again and again. Unfortunately it is oft-times overlooked. Other things become emphasized, such as projects, programs, and the like. We overlook the love of God, the love of Christ, forgiveness, and obedience when we start concentrating on works instead of faith and love.

Oh, that we would continually remember David's prayer as recorded in the Eighty-sixth Psalm,

> *Be merciful unto me, O Lord: for I cry unto thee daily* (all day long).
> *Give ear, O Lord, unto my prayer; and attend to the voice of my supplications.*
> *In the day of my trouble I will call upon thee: for thou wilt answer me.*
> *For thou art great, and doest wondrous things: thou art God alone.*
> *Teach me thy way, O Lord; I will walk in thy truth: unite my heart* (give me singleness of heart) *to fear* (have reverential awe for) *thy name.*
> *I will praise thee, O Lord my God, with all my heart: and I will glorify thy name for evermore.*
> *But thou, O Lord, art a God full of compassion, and gracious, long-suffering, and plenteous in mercy and truth* [Ps. 86:3, 6–7, 10–12, 15].

We are to pray this prayer to God. We should pray that Christ would do these things in us. Remember, if the foundation is not truly laid, then you cannot construct a building to withstand the tests of time.

When considering these thoughts remember the Lord Jesus said,

THOU SHALT LOVE THY NEIGHBOR AS THYSELF [Matt. 22:39].

> *But I say unto you, Love your enemies, bless them that curse you, do good to them that hate you, and pray for them which despitefully* (spitefully) *use you, and persecute you* [Matt. 5:44].

He does not end the statement there. He goes to the heart of the matter, saying, *That ye may be the children* (sons) *of your Father which is in heaven* [Matt. 5:45]. This is part of the foundation. Guess what? We cannot know the breadth, depth, length, and height of Christ's love, *which passeth knowledge* until we are in this foundation, until we are grounded in His love. This attitude toward others, the brethren, the enemies, those who despitefully use us is not natural. We must become a new creature in order to do these things.

We need to ask ourselves the following: Am I loving my enemies? Am I praying for those who curse me and say false things about me? Am I willing to be reconciled to others? Can I honestly love them? Can I truly pray that God will have mercy upon them, and send His Spirit to open their eyes? This is part of the foundation, an important, integral part. These are necessary ingredients if we want to know and enjoy the higher, richer experiences *in Christ*. But the foundation comes first!

Third, our attitude toward the demands and commandments of a life *in Christ* must be guided by love. Have you ever thought that they were onerous or burdensome? Have you ever wondered why they are not taught and preached about more often? The life *in Christ* requires obedience to God's commandments, the Sermon on the Mount, the New Testament Epistles, and the Ten Commandments.

Why? Because they produce *the fruit of the Spirit*. The Psalmist says, *O how I love thy law! I love thy commandments above gold; yea, above fine gold* [Ps. 119:97, 127]. David says, *The law of the Lord is perfect, converting* (restoring) *the soul* [Ps. 19:7]. David continues this psalm, saying,

> . . . *the testimony of the Lord is sure, making wise the simple.*
> *The statutes of the Lord are right, rejoicing the heart: the commandment of the Lord is pure, enlightening the eyes.*
> *The fear of the Lord is clean, enduring forever: the judgments of the Lord are true and righteous altogether.*
> *More to be desired are they than gold, yea, than much fine gold: sweeter also than honey and the honeycomb* (the drippings of the honeycomb) [Ps. 19:7–10].

The words of David say much about God our Father and why we should love Him.

The Apostle John says, *For this is the love of God, that we keep his commandments, and his commandments are not grievous* (burdensome) [1 John 5:3]. People can answer in the affirmative when you ask them if they want to know the love of Christ and want to be filled with the fullness of God. These are easy questions to answer. However, their response to other, harder questions is very important. What is your appraisal of God's commandments as revealed in Scripture? What are your thoughts regarding the requirements for living a Christian life as being too broad or being too narrow? What are your primary guideposts for enjoying life? What are your answers and actions regarding these questions?

There are certain things which the person *in Christ* is not to do, which do not mix with the foundation of this building.

An important part of the foundation of love is not only desiring God's commandments, but loving them and rejoicing in them. The Lord Jesus describes this beautifully in the Sermon on the Mount, saying, *Blessed are they which do hunger and thirst after righteousness: for they shall be filled* [Matt. 5:6]. The people who are going to be filled are those who *hunger and thirst after righteousness* not after blessings. This is a distinct difference in the foundation. Liberty or freedom *in Christ* means that a person hungers and thirsts after righteousness. Philip Dodderidge expressed it beautifully when he said, "[I] Count it my supreme delight to hear thy dictates and obey."

Last, the foundation suggests stability. Our love is to be stable and constant. It is not to be variable or fitful. Our life *in Christ* is to be grounded in love; it is to be founded on love. Further, it is to be like God's love. Remember, our Lord says, *Be ye therefore perfect, even as your Father which is in heaven is perfect* [Matt. 5:48].

Think about God's love. It is perfect, and it is self-generated. It starts from within and goes out to others. That is why God sent His only begotten Son into the world. He did it despite what He saw in the world. He poured out His own self-generated love, a love that originated within Himself, in excessive abundance. How are we to become perfect as our Father in Heaven? Our love is to be the same as our Father's. It must be on a foundation that cannot be moved, shaken, or affected. It must be able to withstand the storms and the tests of life. Therefore, the foundation must be on a rock.

Shakespeare states it appropriately in one of his sonnets,

> *Love is not Love*
> *Which alters when it alteration finds,*
> *Or bends with the remover to remove:*
>
> *O, no! It is an ever fixed mark,*
> *That looks on tempests, and is*
> never shaken;

Agape love does not change. It suffers long, it is not easily provoked, it believes all things, it bears all things, it never fails, it is grounded in love, and it stands on a firm foundation. That wonderful hymn, "How Firm a Foundation," by John Rippon, provides additional insight. Dwell on each verse, each line, and let each thought permeate your heart and mind as you rejoice in so doing.

> *How firm a foundation, ye saints of the Lord,*
> *Is laid for your faith in His excellent word!*
> *What more can He say than to you He hath said,*
> *To you who for refuge to Jesus have fled?*
> *To you who for refuge to Jesus have fled?*
>
> *"Fear not, I am with thee, O be not dismayed,*
> *For I am thy God, I will still give thee aid;*
> *I'll strengthen thee, help thee, and cause thee to stand,*
> *Upheld by My righteous, omnipotent hand,*
> *Upheld by My righteous, omnipotent hand.*
>
> *"When through the deep waters I call thee to go,*
> *The rivers of sorrow shall not overflow;*
> *For I will be near thee, thy troubles to bless.*
> *And sanctify to thee thy deepest distress,*
> *And sanctify to thee thy deepest distress.*
>
> *"The soul that on Jesus hath leaned for repose,*
> *I will not, I will not desert to his foes;*
> *That soul, though all hell should endeavor to shake,*
> *I'll never, no, never, no, never forsake,*
> *I'll never, no, never, no, never forsake."*

"Only a deep love to God can stand up to the trials, stresses, strains, and hazards of life. Belief alone is not enough. It is essential and can take us a long way, but when life's storms and tests come it is not enough. It is love alone that stands and withstands," to quote and paraphrase Martyn Lloyd-Jones.

When we cannot understand, or when we are baffled, or when we cannot explain something, then it is love that holds us up. It is the foundation *rooted and grounded in love* that supports us and in turn will enable us to comprehend with all the saints *the love of Christ, which passeth knowledge*, and to *be filled with all the fullness of God* [Eph. 3:19].

Amen!

14

Receiving Fully

> *May be able to comprehend* (understand) *with all saints what is the breadth* (width), *and length, and depth, and height;*
> *And to know the love of Christ, which passeth knowledge, that ye might be filled with all the fullness of God* [Eph. 3:18–19].

Paul continues his meaningful and enlightening prayer in the eighteenth and nineteenth verses. The previous contents of this prayer lead deliberately and logically to the petitions contained in these verses, which overflow with love, knowledge, and the impact of the Holy Spirit dwelling within a person's heart.

These are interesting and challenging verses. There are many verses in Scripture about which the expositors and commentators have much to say. However there is not much information available on these verses. The subject matter with which we are dealing cannot be easily divided into little categories and examined in a cut-and-dried manner.

In some respects these truths cannot be analyzed and dissected, "just as you cannot analyze and dissect a fragrance," according to Martyn Lloyd-Jones. When approaching these two verses it is safe to say that the first thing you notice is the word *comprehend*.

What does *comprehend* mean as it is used? Webster defines it several ways: "to grasp the meaning mentally, to embrace, and something that comes within the range or scope of a statement whether it is clearly mentioned or not." These definitions clearly imply that *comprehend* is something you initiate on your own and over which you exercise control.

However, when considering the Greek word *katalambanō*, you find that it means "to receive fully," "to lay hold of." What a difference between Webster and Scripture! The one is from within self, whereas the other comes from outside self.

Ruth Paxson provides additional light on the phrase you "*[m]ay be able to comprehend,*—to stretch your mind over so as to grasp with a divine insight and a human response which makes it your own, and this to the limit of an ever-growing mental and spiritual capacity. But only as we are strengthened by the Spirit in the inner man, and as Christ indwells us deeply, can we so comprehend.

"Paul prays that we may be able to comprehend . . . something that is both comprehensible and measurable, yet the petition stops abruptly without telling what it is. May it not be the work of the triune God in our redemption so clearly taught in Ephesians I–III? . . . What could possibly enhance Christ's preciousness to us more than a daily richer comprehension of the measurements of this glorious salvation? For that very purpose may they pass in review before our minds and hearts once more. *The Breadth*—the redeemed. *The Length*—God's eternal purpose from eternity to eternity. *The Depth*—depravity from which the sinner was delivered[;] death in which the sinner was found. *The Height*—position to which [the] saint was raised."

The Apostle is praying that the saints will *receive fully* the breadth, length, depth, and height of *the love of Christ,* and *be filled with all the fullness of God.*

Where does this come from? From outside ourselves.

Paul prays that we will fully receive it. He wants us to grasp it with divine insight. The human response is limited even when growing mentally and spiritually.

One of the highest attainments in our life *in Christ* is to know the love of Christ. How do we get to know the love of someone? By getting to know them. You cannot really get to know someone's love unless you get to know them.

Paxson also provides words of enlightenment regarding the phrase *[t]o know the love of Christ.* "We can know that Christ loved us and gave Himself for us. We can know the faithfulness of His love as manifested in countless ways every day of our lives; its tenderness as it comforts us in suffering and sorrow; its fellowship as it shares with us everything it possesses; its patience as it forgives us the seventy times seven. We can also daily add to our knowledge of the love of Christ as we company with Him in prayer and in the study of his Word; as we fellowship with other saints who know and experience deeply the love of Christ; and as we enter more fully into the fellowship of his sufferings, 'filling up on our part that which is lacking of the afflictions of Christ for his body's sake'" [Col. 1:24]

In these verses the Apostle is praying about Christ's love. He wants the Ephesians to perceive the greatness of Christ's love for them and others who are *in Christ*. As Calvin appropriately states it, "such an apprehension or knowledge springs from faith."

It is appropriate to remember the people to whom Paul is writing and for whom he is praying. They are followers, they have believed the Gospel, and they have realized something of God's love. Yet at this juncture, the Apostle prays that they may *receive fully* this love with all the saints.

There are three factors to consider in this matter: *love*, *saints*, and being *able*. First, there is love and a preliminary awareness of God's love. It can take many forms or have various interpretations. However, the love we are contemplating is much greater than awareness. Those who experience it are tempted to say that they had never known the love of God before. These are people who had known *of it* or *about it*, but did not really *know it*.

Never make the mistake of thinking that because some one professes to be a Christian, or to be *in Christ*, that he or she knows all about the love of God. A person needs to leave the waters edge and explore the depths.

It requires being strengthened by the Spirit in the inner man, and Christ dwelling in us so that we can fully receive *with all saints*. Why does the Apostle pray *with all saints*?

Remember, we are members of the community of believers. No saint or group of saints has the capacity to grasp the whole counsel of God or His eternal purpose. Each one may understand or comprehend in part, but it takes all the saints, *Till we all come in* (into) *the unity of the faith, and of the knowledge of the Son of God, unto a perfect* (mature) *man* [Eph. 4:13].

It takes every saint to enable all the saints to become full grown. Each one needs the strength of the community. We need their help if we are to fully receive our wealth *in Christ*, and have the strength to grasp it.

When realizing we are to fully receive it, we should consider certain important factors. What we are considering in these verses is not a concept, it is Christ's love. It is our personal knowledge of Him and His love. The Apostle John says, *And we have known and believed the love that God hath to us* [1 John 4:16]. This particular verse is equivalent to saying we have known by believing, because such knowledge is perceived only by faith. This is worth repeating: We have known by believing, because such knowledge is perceived only by faith.

An undecided or doubtful opinion is different from faith. John is saying that by faith we know God's love toward us. The Fatherly love is grasped with understanding *in Christ*, and nothing is really known of Christ except by those who are God's children by grace.

The end of all our knowledge should be *to receive fully* the knowledge of Christ's love. As stated before, that is the end, the objective, and the purpose of all doctrine. The New Testament leads one to Christ.

It may be said that most people who know or have known this love of Christ to which Paul refers have been deeply taught and are well-versed in doctrine, but there have always been and there always will be exceptions and thank God that this is true. If you only consider doctrine and stop there, you will not know this love of Christ. You must proceed from doctrine to the Person. All biblical doctrine is about the blessed Person: Jesus Christ. Therefore, you must be ever aware of Him, realizing that doctrine always leads to Him.

Note what the Apostle says to the Philippians,

> *That I may know him, and the power of his resurrection, and the fellowship of his sufferings, being made conformable unto his death* [Phil. 3:10].

> *Brethren, I count not myself to have apprehended: but this one thing I do, forgetting those things which are behind, and reaching forth unto those things which are before,*
> *I press toward the mark for the prize of the high calling of God in Christ Jesus* [Phil. 3:13–14].

The word *apprehend* means "to receive thoroughly." Once you know the Person Jesus Christ you begin to love Him. Then you feel that what you have received is not enough, so you want more and more. Then you want to know Him better, which is to love Him better or more. The more we know Him, the more we know His love toward us. That is where the effort and concentration are to be. How much do we know of Christ's love? How much more do we want to know?

Oh, that we may progress to the heights expressed in that beautiful hymn, "More Love to Thee, O Christ," by Elizabeth Prentiss.

More love to Thee, O Christ, More love to Thee!
Hear Thou the prayer I make On bended knee;
This is my earnest plea,

More love, O Christ, to Thee,
More love to Thee, More love to Thee!

Once earthly joy I craved, Sought peace and rest;
Now Thee alone I seek; Give what is best:
This all my prayer shall be,

Refrain

Then shall my latest breath Whisper Thy praise;
This be the parting cry My heart shall raise;
This still its prayer shall be,

Refrain

Second, there are the *saints*. The eighteenth verse of the third chapter contains the phrase *with all saints*. The word *saint* as it is used means "set apart, separate, holy." "It is a term used for the New Testament followers *in Christ* and reveals that this knowledge is possible only to those believing in the Lord Jesus Christ. The Apostle prayed, *That Christ may dwell in your hearts by faith*," to quote and paraphrase Martyn Lloyd-Jones.

As in previous generations, people today believe these blessings are available only to ministers, priests, or full-time Christian workers, but not to people who are engaged in other occupations or attend worship services on a regular basis.

These ideas are contrary to New Testament teachings. This prayer, this teaching of Paul's, is for all who are *in Christ*, not just a few or some special ones occupying certain positions.

To accept anything short of *with all saints* is to say we do not believe the Word of God, and this is important, it is to say by our actions that we are content with what we have and content to remain in the church as we are.

There is nothing so dishonoring to God, His Son, His Spirit, and His Word as a spirit of self-satisfaction whereby people wish to remain babes *in Christ* and refuse to scale the heights *to receive fully* the love of Christ.

All the saints are to seek more and more understanding whenever or wherever it concerns the love and knowledge of Christ.

The third point is being *able*. We are to acquire a real awareness of Christ's love to each of us. The eighteenth verse reads, *May be able to comprehend*. When we first read this we may interpret it one way. However, it is important to know the proper interpretation. The Greek word for *able* is e*xischuō*, and it means "to have full power," which is entirely different from being able.

The Apostle deliberately provided the extra emphasis. He had already prayed that they would be strengthened, and now he prays that they will *have full power, that they will be thoroughly strong*. What does this mean? We need *to know the love of Christ*. We need to be strengthened; we need to have full power, because of the weight of God's love that we will bear.

Love is powerful and weighty. God is love, and that love contains His might, His majesty, and His power. We need that power *to receive fully* the love of Christ, because love alone recognizes, understands, and receives love. You must have love in your heart if you are going to know it and experience it. Love alone can appreciate love. That is why we must be *rooted and grounded in love* in order to receive it fully.

What does Paul mean by *what is the breadth* (width), *and length, and depth, and height; And to know the love of Christ* [Eph. 3:18]?

The Apostle reminds us that we are dealing with Christ's love to us, not our love to Him. The Apostle's terminology suggests the vastness of Christ's love. "He who knows it (Christ's love) truly and perfectly is in every respect a wise man," as wisely stated by John Calvin.

Wherever people look to the doctrine of salvation they find something related to the love of Christ, and find that Christ's love contains every aspect of wisdom within it.

Think of the phrase this way: that ye may fully receive the love, which is the length, breadth, depth, and height, and is the complete perfection of our wisdom.

Why do we consider this? Because the Apostle admonishes us in this way: it is our responsibility to know whatever is necessary *to receive fully* Christ's love. We should meditate, day and night, upon Christ's love for us. It is there, it is all-sufficient, and it is wherever we go. We cannot go beyond Christ's love without overstepping the lawful bounds of wisdom.

Our chief defect as followers of Christ may be in failing to realize His amazing love and what it can do in us. We spend so much time thinking about so many different things, but so little time in knowing Christ's love and meditating upon it. Let us look at it in the terms the Apostle uses: *breadth* (width), *length*, *depth*, and *height*.

What should we consider in the *breadth* (width) of this love?

> *And I beheld, and I heard the voice of many angels round about the throne and the beasts* (living creatures) *and the elders: and the number of them was ten thousand times ten thousand, and thousands of thousands;*
>
> *Saying with a loud voice, Worthy is the Lamb that was slain to receive power, and riches, and wisdom, and strength, and honor, and glory, and blessing.*
>
> *And every creature which is in heaven, and on the earth, and under the earth, and such as are in the sea, and all that are in them, heard I saying, Blessing, and honor, and glory, and power, be unto him that sitteth upon the throne, and unto the Lamb for ever and ever* [Rev. 5:11–13].

One day we shall see the breadth of Christ's love.

> *Lie not one to another, seeing that ye have put off the old man with his deeds;*
>
> *And have put on the new man, which is renewed in knowledge after the image of him that created him:*
>
> *Where there is neither Greek nor Jew, circumcision nor uncircumcision, Barbarian, Scythian, bond* (slave) *nor free: but Christ is all, and in all* [Col. 3:9–11].

There are to be vast multitudes, and there is to be neither Gentile, nor Jew, nor Barbarian, nor Scythian, nor free.

We are to consider these facts even when realizing we are a minority. The Apostle prays that the Ephesians and we might know the breadth of Christ's love. When we do, we will know that this love, power, and strength is working for us and in us and making things possible when submitting ourselves to Him.

What about the *length* of Christ's love? Length indicates the endlessness of Christ's love. It reminds me of the T-Shirts that the Nike Company put out, saying, "There is no finishing line." In other words, those who run or jog have no finish line. It goes on and on. There is no finishing line to God's love.

The Lord appeared unto Jeremiah and said to him, *Yea, I have loved thee with an everlasting love* [Jer. 31:3]. This term *length* should remind us that God's love in Christ began in eternity and will continue forever. The Reformers, Puritans, and Evangelical leaders of the past were more theologically minded than we. They knew about the love of Christ.

They knew the importance of theology and doctrine. Consequently they spoke and wrote about the Covenant of Redemption and the Covenant of Grace. They knew that before man and the world were created, the Fall of man was foreseen by God. And so an agreement between God the Father and God the Son was made. The Son entered into a covenant with the Father whereby he would save and redeem man—the Covenant of Redemption. And the Father covenanted with the Son to grant privileges and blessings to those who were given to the Son—the Covenant of Grace. They knew that Christ's love was not impetuous and that it did not come into being suddenly.

Christ's love is from everlasting to everlasting. It is unchanging. Scripture says,

> *Jesus Christ the same yesterday, and today, and for ever* [Heb. 13:8].

> THEREFORE *being justified by faith, we have peace with God through our Lord Jesus Christ:*
> *By whom also we have access by faith into this grace wherein we stand, and rejoice in hope of the glory of God.*
> *And not only so, but we glory in tribulations also: knowing that tribulation worketh patience* (produces perseverance);
> *And patience, experience* (character); *and experience, hope:*
> *And hope maketh not ashamed* (does not disappoint); *because the love of God is shed abroad* (has been poured out) *in our hearts by the Holy Ghost which is given unto us* [Rom. 5:1–5].

His love goes on and on, and it goes through all the stages, situations, and conditions of life. It is always there, even though we may at times close our minds and hearts to it.

Nothing can separate us from the love of Christ. Oh, that we would have the faith expressed by Paul, who said,

> *For I am persuaded, that neither death, nor life, nor angels, nor principalities, nor powers, nor things present, nor things to come,*

> *Nor height, nor depth, nor any other creature, shall be able to separate us from the love of God, which is in Christ Jesus our Lord* [Rom. 8:38–39].

What about the *depth* of His love? Paul expresses it meaningfully, saying, Christ

> *Who, being in the form of God, thought it not robbery to be equal with God:*
> *But made himself of no reputation (emptied himself), and took upon him the form of a servant, and was made in the likeness of men:*
> *. . . he humbled himself, and became obedient unto death, even the death of the cross* [Phil. 2:6–8].

When considering the *depth* of His love, it is important to realize what He did and what He suffered.

This brings us to the *height* of His love and to a very important point. Most people tend to think of their salvation only in terms of forgiveness. They limit the love of Christ.

Christ died that we might be given a new birth—not merely to save us from punishment, but to make us children of God, sons of God, heirs of God, and joint heirs with Himself.

Behold, what manner of love the Father hath bestowed upon us, that we should be called the sons of God: Therefore, the world knoweth us not, because it knew him not.

We are to realize what it is to know the love of Christ. We are to be filled with this love and the knowledge of it. The Greek interpretation is that we may have full power *to receive fully* with all the saints the love of Christ.

In summary, the *breadth* is the Jew and Gentile made into one new man in the Body of Christ, the *length* is God's eternal purpose from Alpha to Omega, the *depth* is the depravity from which the sinner was delivered, and the death in which the sinner was found, and the *height* is the position to which the saint has been raised *in Christ*, in the heavenlies, and far above all.

May we receive fully with all the saints the love of Christ and give thanks for it forever and ever.

Amen!

15

Knowing the Love of Christ

May be able to comprehend (understand) *with all saints what is the breadth* (width), *and length, and depth, and height;*
And to know the love of Christ, which passeth knowledge, that ye might be filled with all the fullness of God [Eph. 3:18–19].

After considering *able*, which is to have full power; *comprehend*, which is to receive fully; *apprehend*, which is to receive thoroughly by faith; and the *breadth* (width), *length*, *depth*, and *height* of Christ's love toward us; it is time to proceed to knowing the unknowable, which is *to know the love of Christ, which passeth knowledge.*

These words, phrases, and thoughts are part of the Apostle's prayer to God in behalf of the community of believers in Ephesus. Paul wants them to have an understanding of the nature and character of this knowledge. He does not want them to go astray, but strongly desires that they obtain the proper knowledge. Therefore, he identifies three specific areas.

When considering Paul's prayer, we are to consciously apply these truths to our daily lives. We must conceptualize, since there are different types of knowledge. Therefore, it is appropriate to remind ourselves that there is conceptual knowledge, or the knowledge of concepts and ideas; there is instinctive or intuitive knowledge; and there is common or horse-sense knowledge.

In this instance, we are considering the conceptual type, with emphasis upon applying and using it. Paul does not merely pray for the Ephesians to know that Christ loves them in an elementary way; he prays that they will *know the love of Christ, which passeth knowledge, that ye might be filled with all the fullness of God.* Paul wants them to know much more; he wants them to expand their hearts and minds in order to grasp Christ's immeasurable love. To do this requires effort on our part as well as the power and might of the Holy Spirit. What are we to do? We are to begin by acquiring more knowledge in the following areas by thinking about taking a firm mental grasp and laying hold of something with the mind.

Have you ever had a situation where you tried to learn to do something, but just had a "dickens of a time" grasping the subject matter or in performing the feat? What did you do? Practice, of course, learn the basic rudiments or principles, wrestle with it, and persist.

Basically, it was a mental process, something the mind had to grasp. Paul prays that these followers will grasp *the love of Christ* in their minds.

It is not what Christ had done for them, but what Christ can do in them. There is a difference. It requires practicing, learning, and persisting.

What is meant by grasping *the love of Christ* with your mind? Is there a contradiction? Think about what has been considered: in the realm of love you do not rely upon the intellect; there is the importance of being *rooted and grounded in love*; and love alone comprehends love. It is important to focus on the mental aspects of knowing the love of Christ.

How do we resolve these divergent points? When Paul says he wants us to receive thoroughly the love of Christ, he is not saying it is purely an intellectual process. He recognizes there is always an intellectual aspect to love, and indeed it is an essential part. Unfortunately, the prevailing concept of love is lacking at best and in many respects, is seriously defective.

Usually, in love there is a real intellectual element, an element of understanding. Please note for what Paul prays,

> *And this I pray, that your love may abound yet more and more in knowledge and in all judgment* (discernment);
> *That ye may approve things that are excellent; that ye may be sincere and without offense till the day of Christ;*
> *Being filled with the fruits of righteousness, which are by Jesus Christ, unto the glory and praise of God* [Phil. 1:9–11].

He prays that they may learn to pray from his example and aspire to progress in those gifts. He wants true growth for these followers, which Calvin identifies as "... the true growth of Christians is when they progress in knowledge and (in) understanding and in love . . . For the more we progress in knowledge, the more ought our love to increase."

The meaning Calvin wanted us to grasp is what Paul wanted and the Holy Spirit wants, which is that your love may increase according to the measure of knowledge. Paul means a knowledge that is full and complete. He does not mean knowledge of all things. Paul prays *That ye may approve things that are excellent* [Phil. 3:10]. He wants them to know what is good or expedient, but he does not want their minds filled "with empty subtleties or speculations," as Calvin expressed it.

Love in the New Testament is never intuitive, instinctive, emotional, or irrational. We understand this much better when we accept the truths expressed by the apostles and the emphasis they placed upon *comprehending* and *apprehending*, that this means in *the original to receive fully* and *to receive thoroughly*. Love can be contemplated. Certainly love has a contemplative element to it. Love will make you think. If it does not, then it is just a physical instinct.

The Apostle Paul prays that the Ephesians, with all the saints, will study the love of Christ. His love is to be studied, and the more you study it, the more you enjoy it and the more you want it. What about the people who say they love a subject or topic or something else? The more they know about it, the more they love it.

The Apostle says that our first true response to this love is that we begin "laying hold of it," or grasping it mentally. Our love for Christ increases as we apply our minds and grasp hold. It does not increase by remaining passive, or by ignoring the Person Jesus Christ, or by hoping for some great experience to impact our hearts and our minds some day. We have to apply our minds in order to grasp or lay hold of the concept and to obtain an understanding of Christ's love.

We are to survey, appraise, inspect, scrutinize, and study the Cross and Christ. When we do these things, two items become very apparent: we go into a lot of detail, and we spend a lot of time on it. As a result, we are blessed with *the fruit of the Spirit*.

Next, we are to focus on the phrase *to know the love of Christ*. The word *know* in this verse comes from the Greek word *ginōskō* which means "to understand." It refers to knowledge that is rooted and grounded in personal experience, in a hands-on experience. In this instance, it refers to direct and immediate knowledge. It is not the result of meditating and contemplating.

Once again, note the Apostle's sequence: first, conceptual knowledge, then experiential knowledge. The one should lead to the other. We are to proceed from the external to the internal, from what Christ has done for us to what Christ can do in us.

We are to look at Christ's love with a sense of awe, wonder, and amazement, but we are to experience it, to be filled with it, and to understand it. We are to become fully and completely aware of the fact that Christ loves us fully and completely with an immeasurable love. The New Testament teaches that Christ loves us, forgives us, and has taken our sins upon Himself. We become aware of it, accept it, believe it, and rest upon it. And in many cases, that is exactly what happens. We rest upon it.

But there is more, and thank God there is. We are to know Christ's love. We are to experience it. We are to have it actively working in us. Pray God that this happens to each and everyone of us.

The next term to consider is *which passeth knowledge*. At first glance, this thought seems a little incongruous. However, a closer examination reveals that the Greek word for *passeth* is *huperballō* which means to "surpass," to exceed."

Paul prays *to know the love of Christ, which passeth knowledge*. Though we may come to know the love of Christ, it is in some respects like a never-ebbing sea. It is inexhaustible; it is unsearchable in its entirety. No matter how much we experience it, there is always more. We should always go forward and press onward because the love of Christ pours forth refreshing water from a bottomless well.

There is a question to ponder after examining the three terms we have been considering. Is this knowledge we have been describing available to all followers *in Christ* here and now, or not? There is no question that the Apostle prays that the community of believers in Ephesus will *know the love of Christ* and that they will experience it. Paul believes this and believes it is available to all the saints.

Consider what Peter says,

> *That the trial* (genuineness) *of your faith, being much more precious than of gold that perisheth, though it be tried* (tested) *with fire, might be found unto praise and honor and glory at the appearing* (revelation) *of Jesus Christ:*

> *Whom having not seen, ye love; in whom, though now ye see him not, yet believing, ye rejoice with joy unspeakable and full of glory* [1 Pet. 1:7–8].

We should remind ourselves that Peter focuses attention on Christ by saying *at the appearing* (revelation) *of Jesus Christ*. Calvin reminds us that we are to turn "to Christ if we wish to see glory and praise in our afflictions." Yes, there are trials in our faith, but they have honor and glory *in Christ*. Yet, during those times it is difficult to see.

Then, Peter proceeds to present two truths: ye love Christ whom ye have not seen, and ye believe on Him whom ye have not seen. The former arises from the latter. Faith is the cause of love, because by offering us blessings and happiness He draws us to Himself.

Peter commends the believers to whom he is writing, because they believe in Christ whom they have not seen, and they realize it is the nature of faith to be satisfied with blessings hidden from our sight. Faith is not measured by sight. The eyes of faith are able to penetrate into the invisible kingdom of God. Faith kindles our heart's love to Christ.

Faith has Christ, the Son of God, as its object. Faith goes beyond a mere awareness of Christ. It proceeds to what Christ is to us, what blessings He bestows upon us, and what joy and happiness He gives us.

Further evidence of Christ's love to all the saints is revealed and confirmed in Jesus' own words: *He that hath my commandments, and keepeth them, he it is that loveth me: and he that loveth me shall be loved of my Father, and I will love him, and will manifest* (reveal) *myself to him* [John 14:21]. Jesus prays in His high priestly prayer *that the world may know thou hast sent me, and hast loved them, as thou hast loved me* [John 17:23]. These passages provide direct, immediate knowledge of Christ's love for us and to us. There is no mistake about it. It is for us to know what has been revealed.

This love was made known to the disciples, to the apostles, and to individuals throughout the ages. Charles Wesley wrote that beautiful hymn, "Jesus, Lover of My Soul."

> *Jesus, Lover of my soul,*
> *Let me to thy bosom fly.*

Wesley also wrote,

> *Thou, O Christ, art all I want;*
> *More than all in Thee I find.*

Edward Payson, a minister in the early 1800s wrote,

> "O if ministers only saw the inconceivable glory that is before them, and the preciousness of Christ, they would not be able to refrain from going about leaping and clapping their hands for joy and exclaiming, "I'm a minister of Christ!" When I read Bunyan's description of the land of Beulah where the sun shines and the birds sing day and night I used to doubt whether there were such a place. But now my own experience has convinced me of it, and it infinitely transcends all my previous conceptions."

Payson also wrote the following near the end of his life,

> "Christians might avoid much trouble and inconvenience if they would only believe what they profess, that God is able to make them happy without anything else. They imagine that if such a dear friend were to die, or if such blessings were to be removed, they would be miserable, whereas God can make them a thousand times happier without them. To mention my own case, God has been depriving me of one blessing after another (he was on his death bed when he wrote this), but as each one was removed He has come in and filled its place. And now, when I am a cripple and not able to move, I am happier than ever I was in my life before or ever expected to be; and if I had believed this twenty years ago I might have been spared much anxiety."

Pray God that we might know the personal love of Jesus Christ.

We are to survey these truths, examine them in detail, and spend time studying them. Why? *To know* (understand) *the love of Christ, which surpasseth knowledge.*

May I leave you with the following, which has been described by some as the most beautiful English hymn ever written? It is "When I Survey the Wondrous Cross," by Isaac Watts, a prolific composer of hymns.

> *When I survey the wondrous cross*
> *On which the Prince of Glory died,*
> *My richest gain I count but loss,*
> *And pour contempt on all my pride.*
>
> *Forbid it, Lord, that I should boast,*
> *Save in the death of Christ my God:*
> *All the vain things that charm me most,*
> *I sacrifice them to His blood.*

See, from His head, His hands, His feet,
Sorrow and love flow mingled down:
Did e'er such love and sorrow meet,
Or thorns compose so rich a crown?

Were the whole realm of nature mine,
That were a present far too small;
Love so amazing, so divine,
Demands my soul, my life, my all.

Amen!

16

The Supreme Need

> *May be able to comprehend* (understand) *with all saints what is the breadth* (width), *and length, and depth, and height;*
> *And to know the love of Christ, which passeth knowledge, that ye might be filled with all the fullness of God* [Eph. 3:18–19].

Certain questions seem appropriate when contemplating Paul's statement that the Ephesians

> *May be able to comprehend* (understand) *with all saints what is the breadth* (width), *and length, and depth, and height;*
> *And to know the love of Christ, which passeth knowledge, that ye might be filled with all the fullness of God* [Eph. 3:18–19].

How can we attain the knowledge available to us? How can our love for Jesus Christ continue to grow and grow? How do we progress from the belief that our sins and sinfulness have been forgiven to becoming new creatures in Christ Jesus? How are we capable of handling, thinking, and doing differently in daily situations that confront us, test us, try us, frustrate us, exasperate us, and rob us of much joy we would otherwise possess? Whether we admit it or not, when Jesus Christ and the Holy Spirit enter into our hearts, minds, and souls we are "restless until we find our rest in Him," as St. Augustine stated. The New Testament addresses these questions, not just on the surface, but in depth.

The person believing he or she is forgiven and going to heaven will find, upon further examination, that such a thought pattern or attitude rejects much of the Lord's teaching and deprives us of the fullness of the relationship we should have with Him and God the Father.

> *Let that therefore abide in you, which ye have heard from the beginning. If that which ye have heard from the beginning shall remain in you, ye also shall continue in the Son, and in the Father.*
>
> *And this is the promise that he hath promised us, even eternal life.*
>
> *These things have I written unto you concerning them that seduce (try to deceive) you.*
>
> *But the anointing which ye have received of him abideth in you, and ye need not that any man teach you: but as the same anointing teacheth you of all things, and is truth, and is no lie, and even as it hath taught you, ye shall abide in him.*
>
> *And now, little children, abide in him; that, when he shall appear, we may have confidence, and not be ashamed before him at his coming.*
>
> *If ye know that he is righteous, ye know that every one that doeth* (practices) *righteousness is born of him* [1 John 2:24–29].

The Apostle John "exhorts us to obedience and describes its fruit as abiding in the Son and the Father, because that which ye have heard will abide in you. John urges us to a steadfast faith and to keep the things we have learned in our hearts. He states that those to whom he was writing had been properly taught in the pure Gospel of Christ, and they should remain in it.

"John points out several truths in this exhortation. By persevering, God's truth abides in them and they abide in God. The one who makes the greatest headway is the one who truly cleaves to God. Sound teaching is highly commended since it unites us to God and it contains the ingredients for truly enjoying Him. We have substantial happiness when God dwells in us, and we truly live when the seed of life conceived in our minds is nourished.

"John emphasizes that *in Christ* is the beginning, the growth, and the perfection of the blessed life. It is not possible outside of Christ, but some people delight in wandering from the Gospel's simple teachings.

"Why did John do this? Because it is necessary for the Spirit of God to direct us in all things. Yes, we may within our finite capabilities have understanding and judgment, but God through His Spirit needs to speak within us," according to John Calvin's exposition.

John says, *ye need not that any man teach you* [1 John 2:27]. He does not ascribe to us wisdom from the teachings of man. "It is the Word of God that furnishes the believer with knowledge, (and wisdom) which the Spirit makes relevant and applicable in the believers life," as described in *The King James Study Bible*.

Calvin continues to expound upon the Apostle John's words stating "for the apostle dwells on the point that believers should keep the pure knowledge of Christ and should not try to reach God any other way." This is as true today as it was when the Apostle John wrote the letter

Calvin provides additional clarity with the following expression, ". . . he clearly shows that the children of God are enlightened by the Spirit simply so that they may know Christ. So long as they did not turn aside from Christ, he promised them the fruit of perseverance, even that they should have boldnesses and not be ashamed at His presence. For faith is not a naked and frigid apprehension of Christ, but a living and real sense of His power that begets confidence. But the nature of confidence is best expressed when he says that it can boldly bear the presence of Christ. . . . But a godly confidence rests on the sight of God alone. That is why the godly calmly wait for Christ and do not dread His presence."

The Apostle says that the believers who taught by the Spirit understood what they were teaching, but that everyone understood according to his or her measure. In some the measure was small, in some it was in the middle, but in none was it perfect. Therefore, there was not one who did not need to progress. All needed to do so.

This doctrine allows us to progress and to consider other truths. When a person understands what is necessary to progress in faith, he or she should continue to thirst and hunger after righteousness in order to become more established in it. This was true of John, Peter, James, Paul, Luke, Matthew, Mark, and all the other saints through the ages.

When John declares that they were taught all things by the Spirit, we must consider it in the context of these verses. He wanted to strengthen their faith and have them progress in it. He wanted to remind them that the Holy Spirit "is the only fit critic and approver of doctrine," as Calvin declared. It is the Spirit that actually seals these truths in our hearts and minds.

How can these truths be sealed? Think of it this way: faith must look to God; God alone can witness to Himself; and the power of the Holy Spirit is required for us to be able, or to have full power, to receive the truths, and to convince our hearts of what we have heard.

The Apostle John says, *but as the same anointing teacheth you of all things, and is truth, and is no lie, and even as it hath taught you, ye shall abide in him* [1 John 2:27]. The Spirit seals the truth that God presents to us. This passage reveals that God rules us and reveals to us with both discernment and judgment, so that we will not be deceived by falsehoods as we progress in faith. The Apostle, under the influence of the Holy Spirit, urges the followers to abide *in Christ*. The words of the Apostle John are revealing and comforting as he states,

> *But the anointing which ye have received of him abideth in you, and ye need not that any man teach you: but as the same anointing teacheth you of all things, and is truth, and is no lie, and even as it* (Holy Spirit) *hath taught you, ye shall abide in him* [1 John 2:27].

Why does the Apostle dwell on this point? It is very simple, and yet it is all encompassing. Believers are to obtain pure knowledge of Christ and His teachings. There is no other way by which they can come to God and know Him.

The Apostle John presents a great truth. Christ's followers are enlightened by the Spirit for one simple and great reason: so that they may know Christ. He promised that the fruit of their perseverance would be boldness and that they would not be ashamed of His presence. Faith is not apprehensive about Christ, but has a living and vital sense of His presence and His power, which begets confidence. How true this is! Faith must be fixed upon Christ and, in turn, is supported by His power, which produces confidence. This confidence boldly bears the presence of Christ. Those who have faith and in whom faith increases calmly wait for Christ and rejoice in His presence.

John closes this portion of his letter by saying, *If ye know that he is righteous, ye know that every one that doeth righteousness is born of him.* John believes "that faith is joined to a holy and pure life," as revealed and declared by John Calvin. The Apostle teaches that no one is born of Christ except those living or striving to live righteously. Those born of Christ are renewed by His Spirit.

The Lord wants us to grow in our knowledge and love of Christ and for our faith in Him to grow. He wants us to apply this knowledge, love, and faith to our daily living, to the ups and downs, to the good and bad, and to the easy and difficult. The Lord Jesus wants to show His grace to others through us during all the different circumstances that we may have to face, endure, and enjoy.

Therefore, we are to know this love of Christ, which surpasseth knowledge. We will deal with this throughout the remaining chapters of Ephesians, especially when dealing with matters concerning conduct and behavior. That is one of the best ways of learning how to achieve an increasing knowledge of the love of Christ.

There are certain negative and positive factors to consider as we continue exploring the eighteenth and nineteenth verses. The first is the negative. We are never to think of the love of Christ and the knowledge of it in mechanical terms. In other words, it is not a case of pressing a button, and something happens. It is not automatic.

It is not a case of reading a book or a portion of Scripture, or doing certain things which other people may have done, and then having a momentous experience or revelation. Just because someone else had an experience in a certain way does not mean God will reveal truths to us in the same manner. We could travel the road to Emmaus or Damascus for a thousand years and never have the same experiences as those two men or Paul. God reveals Himself to us where and when he will.

We need to realize that God's revelations are entirely in His hands and according to His plans. He dispenses His blessings when, where, and how He wishes. It is not a case of doing something and then receiving a prize or payment. It is not a case whereby if we do something, we will receive a free pass, or a specific request will be granted.

We should recognize that books, manuals, and other material might be helpful in our devotional lives. However, we must be aware of the possibility of allowing this to introduce a mechanical thought process.

What are a few positive factors contributing to increasing progressively in our knowledge, our love, and our faith? Mark relates the incident of Bartimaeus, the blind man, calling to Jesus and saying, *Jesus, thou son of David, have mercy on me* [Mark 10:47]. What did Bartimaeus do? He placed himself in Jesus' way. He knew where to find Him; he cried out to Jesus; he came to Jesus immediately when he was called; he obeyed; he did not hesitate; and immediately *he received his sight, and followed Jesus in the way* [Mark 10:52].

What must we do to put ourselves in His way? First, we should pray for ourselves without ceasing. Remember Paul's prayer *That he would grant you, according to the riches of his glory, to be strengthened with might by his Spirit in the inner man* [Eph. 3:16]. Prayer is essential. We should develop a dependence upon prayer and a joyful desire to be in the presence of God. This is important.

A positive attitude toward prayer is the source of great strength. We should always remember the Son of God being tempted in the wilderness. The closer we come to God, the more we will be tempted and tried. Satan does not want us to grow in the Spirit or to grow *in Christ*. He wants us to remain babes in the faith. He does not want us to progress and become mature followers.

Why should we pray? Why should we want to be strengthened? After our Lord Jesus Christ was baptized He was tempted, severely tempted. The more we seek Christ the knowledge and reality of His love, the more we shall be tempted. Scripture speaks of *the wiles* (schemes) *of the devil* [Eph. 6:11] and *the fiery darts of the wicked* (one) [Eph. 6:16].

We need the strength of the Holy Spirit to sustain us and strengthen us. We will have temptations; we will be tested and tried. The more we grow in the Spirit, the more this will happen. Therefore, we need to be strengthened in the Spirit. The Apostle Paul says in the sixth chapter of Ephesians, *we wrestle not against flesh and blood, but against principalities, powers, against the rulers of the darkness of this world* (age), *against spiritual wickedness in high places* [Eph. 6:12]. In some little way, we are following in the Master's footsteps. He was tempted in a way that makes it very difficult to grasp the magnitude of those temptations.

Second, we must learn to seek the Lord Jesus Christ Himself. Yes, ideas, truths, doctrines, theology, and happenings are all important. They contribute to our knowledge and our understanding. But we are to know the Person, the Lord Jesus Christ. We are to seek after Him; we are to develop a personal relationship with Him. Paul says, *that I may know him, and the power of his resurrection* [Phil. 3:10]. Everything we are to learn should lead us to the Person Himself. We are not to be content with knowing facts about the Lord Jesus, or ideas or truths about Him; we are to come to know Him in a personal way.

When we say we are to seek the Lord Himself, what do we mean? We are not to seek experiences or emotional events. We are to seek the Lord Himself.

There are those who thrive on doing something in their church and being constantly involved in activities. They always want to be doing something. However, they do not seek more and more knowledge of the Lord Jesus, nor do they seek to know the love of Christ and grow in that love *which surpasseth knowledge*. They go to meetings, they do things, but they do not grow closer to Christ.

We must not allow meetings, books, or works to interfere with our coming to know Christ and loving Him. We are to seek the Lord Himself.

Remember, the life *in Christ* is not simply a matter of adopting ideas, or thinking everything is fine because my sins are forgiven. It is not a philosophy, or a collection of thoughts and concepts. The special glory and the unique aspect of the life *in Christ* is that we can apply a teaching, but more importantly we get to know that Person and we can walk with Him. It is a Person. It is an individual. We are to reach the point where we can honestly say we know Christ Himself.

The real question is: How do we get to know Him? We are to be ready as the five wise virgins. When He reveals Himself, we are to be as Bartimaeus was. We are to pray, we are to seek to know Him, and we are to realize the presence of Christ. Why? Because we cannot know the love of Christ until we know Christ Himself.

At this time, it is wise to remind ourselves that probably the greatest danger confronting the organized church and the community of believers is not realizing that the love of Christ is our supreme need. Instead, we spend our time and energy in organizing or participating in activities. Then we wonder why so little happens, even though we seem so busy. However, the fact that so little happens should not surprise us. Why is this true? Because we either forget or relegate to a secondary position the true motive and the real energizing power. We should not work as Christians because it is right to do so; we should work because of Christ's love.

Third, we are to continually remind ourselves that the Lord Jesus Christ wants to dwell with us. The Apostle John records Him saying, *Behold, I stand at the door, and knock: if any man hear my voice, and open the door, I will come in to him, and will sup* (dine) *with him, and he with me* [Rev. 3:20].

Think, Christ is saying, *Behold, I stand at the door, and knock*. Note, he does not barge in, he does not pass by, and he does not remain silent. The Lord Jesus continues, saying, *if any man hear my voice, and open the door, I will come in to him, and will sup* (dine) *with him, and he with me*. He will have fellowship, and He will be with us. Do we realize Christ is with us when we are confronted by tests, trials, and temptations?

Paul admonishes the Corinthians, asking, *Know ye not that your bodies are the members of Christ* [1 Cor. 6:15]? He tells them they are not to be joined to harlots, that they are joined to Christ as one spirit. They are to flee fornication. Then Paul asks a penetrating question, *What? Know ye not that your body is the temple of the Holy Ghost which is in you, which ye have of God, and ye are not your own?* Then Paul forcefully reminds them, *For ye are bought with a price: therefore glorify God in your body, and in your spirit, which are God's* [1 Cor. 6:19–20]. In these verses, Paul deals with the practical problem of sinning in the body. Note what he does. He does not indulge in a vague moral teaching or give a lecture or make a general appeal.

What does he do? He reminds them that their bodies are temples and that the Holy Ghost dwells within them. The Holy Ghost is involved in whatever you do with your body. Certainly, there is a sense in which the whole secret of sanctification is to know how and when to utter the word *What?* as Paul did.

When tempted, tried, or tested, remember Paul asking, *What?* It is unthinkable to succumb because the Holy Ghost dwells within you. We are to remind ourselves of this truth. We are to live believing the Lord Jesus Christ loves us and dwells within us.

Fourth, we are to actively and positively seek His love. This point is stressed in the Old Testament as well as in the New Testament. Consider:

> *As the hart panteth (deer longs for) after the water brooks, so panteth my soul after thee, O God.*
> *My soul thirsteth for God, for the living God: when shall I come and appear before God* [Ps. 42:1–2]?

> *Because thy loving-kindness is better than life, my lips shall praise thee* [Ps. 63:3].

> *For a day in thy courts is better than a thousand. I had rather be a doorkeeper* (stand at the threshold) *in the house of my God, than to dwell in the tents of wickedness* [Ps. 84:10].

There is one thing that is true of everyone. We like to be told by word and deed that those whom we love, love us. Actions alone are not sufficient; we like to be told. We like to know that He has loved us with an everlasting love.

Fifth, we are to read the Word of God regularly. The Word has been given to reveal the Lord Jesus Christ to us. This is true of both the Old Testament and the New Testament.

> *And beginning at Moses and all the prophets, he expounded unto them in all the scriptures the things concerning himself* [Luke 24:27].

> *And he said unto them, These are the words which I spake unto you, while I was yet with you, that all things must be fulfilled, which were written in the law of Moses, and in the prophets, and in the psalms, concerning me.*
>
> *Then opened he their understanding, that they might understand the scriptures, . . .* [Luke 24:44–45].

How we read Scripture is important. It is not to be done mechanically, nor is it sufficient for us to say we do so everyday. When reading Scripture we should employ every bit of our intelligence and inquisitiveness. We should pray for the illumination and inspiration of the Holy Spirit. We should concentrate upon what we are doing. The Bible requires concentrating on our capabilities and our faculties. It is a good idea to ask a few questions when beginning to read Scripture. What do I expect? What is my objective? Why am I reading? Why did God through the Holy Spirit inspire this portion of Scripture? What is God saying? How can I come to know Christ and His love? Remember, God continues to speak through His Holy Word.

We have heard and read of people who have had significant experiences or obtained a deeper understanding while reading their Bibles. This has happened to people who have learned to read Scripture in a thoughtful and meditative way. It is not easy to meditate and concentrate. It requires effort, discipline, and strength. Therefore, we need to develop this strength, just as Paul did by praying,

> *That he would grant you, . . . to be strengthened with might by his Spirit in the inner man* [Eph. 3:16].

Scripture has been given to help us. However, it is our responsibility to apply what we read and to learn from it.

A true reading of the Bible requires thought, meditation, contemplation, and preparation. In addition, it involves expectancy and eager anticipation. We are to look for Him and to be ready for Him as He reveals Himself to us. We are to know Christ, to increase our knowledge of Him, and to grow in our love of Him all the days of our life. This is the supreme need!

Amen!

17

Filled With God's Fullness

And to know the love of Christ, which passeth knowledge, that ye might be filled with all the fullness of God [Eph. 3:19].

"This is the doctrinal meaning of the fullness of God, but what does it mean tangibly and practically in relationship to the Church and to the Christian? Is it not just all that vast wealth stored in Christ out of which God draws for the achievement of His purpose (3:11); the fulfillment of His good pleasure (1:9); the carrying out of the counsels of His own will (1:11); the manifestation of the riches of His grace and glory (1:7; 3:15); the working of his mighty power (1:19); the expression of the richness of His mercy and the greatness of His love (2:4)? Is it not also those unsearchable riches in Christ which the saint appropriates for the satisfaction of every Spirit-inspired desire; for the supply of every need of the spirit, soul and body; for the sustenance of life on the highest plane in Christ in the heavenlies, far above all; and for the strength to stand and withstand in the warfare with Satan?" according to these appropriately asked questions by the inimitable Ruth Paxson.

Now it is time to focus attention on "*And to know the love of Christ, which passeth knowledge, that ye might be filled with all the fullness of God.*" What a climax to Paul's meaningful, beautiful prayer *that ye might be filled with all the fullness of God*. The thought, the petition is overwhelming. At first we may say, "Wonderful!" and proceed to the doxology in the last two verses. However, if we pause even for a moment, questions begin to flow in our hearts and minds:

- What does he mean?
- How can it be possible?

- What can I do?
- What impact will it have?

A good place to start in considering this staggering petition is with the original Greek and Scripture. The Greek word for *filled* is *plēroō*, and the Greek word for *fullness* is *plērōma*. To expand upon it, *plēroō* means "complete" or "to fill up" or "to fill full."

Paul says in Colossians, *And ye are complete in him*, . . . [Col. 2:10] or ye are filled up in Him, or filled full in Him. When meditating upon the previous verse [Col. 2:9], you realize it says that He who was "full of grace" (*For in him dwelleth all the fullness of the Godhead bodily*) has imparted that grace to others. The word "For verifies the assertion in verse eight that the heretics' "philosophy" is in accord with the tradition of men and not with Christ or in line with Christian doctrine. This is done by stating that the whole of the divine nature (all the fullness of the Godhead) dwells in Jesus in bodily form. This refutes the Colossian heresy denying the son's full deity and that He possessed a body that could die and make atonement for sin" as noted in the King James Study Bible. This also reaffirms today and in the years to come that *in Him,* (Christ) *dwelleth all the fullness of the Godhead bodily.* How Great thou art!

Previously Paul said, *For it pleased the Father that in him should all fullness dwell* [Col. 1:19], which expresses essentially the same idea. Namely, it was the good pleasure of the Father that in Him (Christ) should all fullness dwell, and in Him dwelleth all the fullness of the Godhead bodily.

In these two verses, Paul describes the fullness of divine grace that is *in Christ*, and tells us that by and through Him it is made available to believers. In this verse [Eph. 3:19], the fullness is the fullness which God has in Christ, since neither individually nor collectively can a person or group ever be filled with all the fullness of God. Paul prays that we may be filled up completely with the divine grace that is in Christ alone, with the fullness that has its source in God only.

Earlier in considering this prayer we noticed the word *that* introduced four significant petitions. This is the fourth one. As we begin contemplating the meaning of this particular phrase, it is well to realize that

- Paul is reaching the heights of his prayer;
- he formulated it step by step, rising ever higher and higher;
- he earnestly prays his desire for the Ephesians;

Filled With God's Fullness

- he was not satisfied with the believers as they were;
- he wanted them to know the unsearchable riches;
- he wanted them to move beyond the beginnings of their faith;
- he wanted them to realize the infinite possibilities; and
- he wanted them to know and to enjoy a personal relationship with Christ Jesus.

In addition, we should remember that an unknown author proclaimed that "the perfection of man consists in his being full of God." The Apostle wants us to be enlightened, strengthened, rooted and grounded, and having full power *to receive fully* to know the love of God. And at the climax of this prayer, he petitions that we *might be filled with all the fullness of God*.

The words *fill* and *full* play a prominent role in Paul's letter.

> *Which is his body, the fullness of him that filleth all in all* [Eph. 1:23].

> *And to know the love of Christ, which passeth knowledge, that ye might be filled with all the fullness of God* [Eph. 3:19].

> *He that descended is the same also that ascended up far above all heavens, that he might fill* (fulfill) *all things* [Eph. 4:10].

> *And be not drunk with wine, wherein is excess* (dissipation); *but be filled with the Spirit* [Eph. 5:18].

Paul, who knew the Lord Jesus Christ, wants the followers of Christ to be filled with His divine grace. He states the objective eloquently and succinctly, saying,

> *Till we all come in* (into) *the unity of the faith, and of the knowledge of the Son of God, unto a perfect* (mature) *man, unto the measure of the stature of the fullness of Christ* [Eph. 4:13].

"The Holy Spirit strengthens us in the inner man that Christ may dwell in every corner and cranny of our lives, thus emptying us of self and enthroning Christ in us as a living reality. He strengthens us that we may comprehend more fully the measurable love of Christ expressed in salvation, and that we may know the unknowable love that made Him our Saviour, thus making Christ so precious to us that we are satisfied in Him! But Satan is always at work to destroy the work of the Spirit and to win us back to allegiance to himself. There is but one safeguard to his cunning wiles; to be filled with Christ that all such temptation be resisted, and that we may in all things and at all times be more than conquerors," as beautifully and forthrightly stated by Ruth Paxson.

The Holy Spirit wants to get rid of the weaknesses, the evil thoughts that exist in our hearts and minds, and replace them with the strength of the Lord Jesus Christ. He wants us strengthened so that we may overcome and resist the cunning evils of Satan.

When considering this beautiful, powerful phrase it is well to know what it is not saying, or even implying. Why should we do this? So we will not misinterpret Scripture. For example, there are some who think they may become lost or dissolved in God, or that they are absorbed by God, and as a consequence lose their personal identity. Some accept Pantheism and believe that God is in everything and in a sense everything is in God; the distinction between God and man is lost and the two become one.

Others teach that man proceeds through various levels or gradations. And still others say Paul was carried away by his own eloquence or was lost in himself. Or they say what Paul meant by this phrase was "that you may be filled with all the various blessings, which God can give to the believing Christian," referring to the blessings bestowed upon individual believers.

All of these teachings contradict Scripture. They are to be rejected.

This petition is the final step in this magnificent prayer. It means what it says, *that ye might be filled with all the fullness of God*. In examining this phrase, one thing should be clear. It is impossible for a person to contain all the fullness of God.

However, some fanatics through the ages have made this claim. It is impossible for a person to be as God. Adam's original sin occurred because man was tempted by that possibility. Satan suggested that God was unfair to the man and woman, that He was keeping them down, and that it was possible for them to become as gods and become equal to God.

When considering this matter and the questions regarding the fullness of God, we should recognize that the attributes of God are divided into two categories: the ones that are not communicable and the ones that are communicable to man. The distinction between the two should allow us to obtain a key understanding of the phrase *that ye might be filled with all the fullness of God*.

Filled With God's Fullness   147

If it were true that the whole of God may dwell in us, then it would probably be true that whatever is true of God would be true of us. However, the attributes of God that are not communicable make it very clear that what is true of God cannot be true of us. What attributes of God are not communicable? They are:

- His eternity, because God is from everlasting to everlasting;
- His immutability, because God cannot change;
- His omnipresence, because God is everywhere;
- His omniscience, because God knows everything;
- His omnipotence, because God's power has no limit; and
- His blessedness, because God possesses absolute blessedness.

We are not to interpret this phrase by saying that these incommunicable attributes of God can dwell in any person, because they cannot.

Christ shows His humility in voluntarily leaving the Godhead and taking the form of man. His humility consisted in abusing Himself, and as Calvin said, "He moved from the highest pinnacle of glory to the lowest ignominy." He emptied Himself!

The *fullness of God* in this passage means "His Majesty." From the beginning Christ had His glory with the Father, as noted in Jesus' prayer: *And now, O Father, glorify thou me with* (alongside) *thine own self with the glory which I had with thee before the world was* [John 17:5]. For in the wisdom of God, before Christ humbled Himself, He was accorded magnificence worthy of God. He had a perfect right to show Himself equal with God. It was lawful and right for Him to do so. It was not wrong for Him to appear to be equal with God.

What are the communicable attributes of God? They are the ones given to man by the grace of God. One is holiness: God is holy, yet He commands us to be holy. *But as he which hath called you is holy, so be ye holy in all manner of conversation* (conduct): *Because it is written, BE YE HOLY; FOR I AM HOLY* [1 Pet. 1:15–16].

Another is righteousness: it is from God. *For the fruit of the Spirit is in all goodness and righteousness and truth* [Eph. 5:9]. Goodness, love, mercy, compassion, loving kindness, long-suffering and faithfulness are communicable attributes. *But the fruit of the Spirit is love, joy, peace, long-*

suffering, gentleness (kindness), *goodness, faith* (faithfulness), *Meekness, temperance* (self-control): *against such there is no law* [Gal. 5:22–23].

These teachings enable us to begin understanding the truth regarding *the fullness of God*. We are to examine not only the blessings of God, but what is said about *the fullness of God*.

How does this fullness become part of us, part of our being? How do we possess it? It happens in and through our Lord and Saviour Jesus Christ. The fullness of which Paul speaks is ours through Christ indwelling in our hearts, and is due to our knowledge of His love.

The Apostle's prayer is most revealing as we examine it. He prays that Christ may dwell in their hearts. If that does not happen then it is impossible to *be filled with all the fullness of God*. When Christ dwells in our hearts, and we begin to know the love of Christ, then *the fullness of God* begins to enter our hearts and minds. Scripture confirms this by preserving for our edification that *Jesus answered and said unto him, If a man love me, he will keep my words: and my Father will love him, and we will come unto him, and make our abode* (home) *with him* [John 14:23].

The significant phrases in this verse are: *If a man love me, he will keep my words, my father will love him, we will come unto him,* and we will *make our abode* (home) *with him*. Paul says this is possible and prays that it will happen. It is practical; it is not abstract. Paul prays that the members of the community of believers will know and experience it.

The doctrine is that in our Lord and Saviour Jesus Christ *dwelleth all the fullness of the Godhead bodily*. What does this mean? If He dwells in our hearts then we will be filled with all the fullness of God. This is God's purpose. It means, as Paul tells the Ephesians,

> *That we henceforth be no more children, tossed to and fro, and carried about with every wind of doctrine, by the sleight* (trickery) *of men, and cunning craftiness . . . .*
> *But speaking the truth in love, may grow up into him in all things, which is the head, even Christ* [Eph. 4:14–15].

These verses present a basic, essential, and complete doctrine of living *in Christ*. It goes well beyond being converted and knowing your sins are forgiven, or being content with life as a babe. It means entering into a mature, full life *in Christ*, and developing *unto the measure of the stature of the fullness of Christ*. It means we are *not* to remain babes *in Christ*.

How do these things work in practice? The New Testament tells us that when we are joined to Christ, we are *in Christ*. *For we are members of his body, of his flesh, and of his bones* [Eph. 5:30].

The Lord Jesus says, *I am the vine, ye are the branches: He that abideth in me, and I in him, the same bringeth forth much fruit: for without me ye can do nothing* [John 15:5]. May this help us understand how we are filled with the fullness of God.

You may wish to think of it in the following way. The whole of my life and my being is in my little finger because of the different organs and parts with relationship to the whole body. They are all living parts. The fullness of my head, heart, and being are in my little finger. I could say the fullness of my life is in my little finger, because while it is a part of my body, my fullness is in it.

When thinking of the fullness of God within us, we should think in terms of quality, not quantity. If Christ is in me, then the fullness of God is in me with respect to the quality of life. The amount may vary from person to person, but the quality is there, and we can all receive of God's fullness.

The gifts may differ; the graces may differ by person. Yet God is always the same. However, the fullness of God in each of us may vary, for we are not identical in every respect. You may have two people who have accepted Christ and are his followers; one may be brilliant and the other ordinary. However, both can be filled with the fullness of God. The fullness does not turn the ordinary person into a genius. His gifts will remain as they were. But, because of his relationship to Christ, the fact that Christ is in him, he is filled with the fullness of God.

What really matters is not the quantity or amount but the quality of our relationship to Christ in experiencing His love. It does not mean that we immediately become divine, that we become eternal, immutable, absolute, omnipotent, and omniscient. It does mean that the communicable attributes of God can and will enter into us.

What we manifest and display are the communicable attributes of God. We will love our enemies, pray for those who hate us, forgive others, and pray for others. Someday we will become mature *in Christ* and attain *unto the measure of the stature of the fullness of Christ*.

May God so bless us.
Amen!

18

Being in Christ

> *And to know the love of Christ, which passeth knowledge, that ye might be filled with all the fullness of God* [Eph. 3:19].

While continuing to examine this verse, there are certain thoughts to keep in mind. Paul was an evangelist, a teacher, and a pastor. He had an excellent mind. He was a sound, rational thinker, and was not controlled by emotion. Paul did not subscribe to fantasies. He was practical and committed to factual data.

There is a question to ponder: when a person is *in Christ* how should he or she approach the realities of life and everyday living? Consider the realities of Paul's prayer. It proceeds from the foundation to one illuminating and strengthening level after another:

- *Bow my knees,*
- *According to the riches of his glory, to be strengthened,*
- *That Christ may dwell in your hearts by faith,*
- *That ye, being rooted and grounded in love,*
- *Might be filled with all the fullness of God*

[Selections from Eph. 3:14–17, 19].

How glorious that is!

There is a great lesson contained in this prayer. When and if we desire to do things for God and Christ, first we should make certain that we are filled with the fullness of God. We should not begin by acting, but by preparing.

The Apostle Paul provides an excellent example. Before embarking upon His ministry he spent three years in preparation. He did not begin to act immediately after his conversion. This is in contrast to the modern slogans or approaches of giving the new converts something to do or electing them to responsible offices.

What is more practical than experience and preparation? The truly practical person is not the one bustling about and rushing from thither to yon. The person being used by the Holy Spirit needs the fullness of God. Then he can become a powerful disciple.

The following statement by an unknown author should be considered: "Religion seems to be part of the unexamined and largely unused background of life." The writer was referring to members of the church. He was pointing out that their religion or faith was in the background of their lives, not in the center or forefront. The writer went on to say, "To the vast majority it can be compared with the knowledge that in an emergency you dial a certain number and help will be instantly available." To these people, religion or faith is only for emergencies and temporary relief, not to be practiced and used on a daily basis.

Faith in Christ is not some reserve you can fall back on, or merely a refuge in time of trouble. It is not to be "unused" or "unexamined." Questions to examine are: Can we relate to Paul's prayer for the Ephesians? Are we concerned with its contents? Is this our prayer? Is this prayer and are these thoughts at the forefront of our minds?

If we answer these questions in the affirmative, then we need to ask: What does it mean in practice, in everyday living? What is true of the person filled with all the fullness of God?

God dwells in them in such a way that He controls them and their faculties. God controls their life, thinking, feelings, and outward actions. God controls their minds, hearts, and will. When filled with the fullness of God, it means that He controls everything about us: the heart, mind, feelings, sensibilities, will, actions, and activities.

What about our thinking? Is it dominated by God? Paul states,

> *I BESEECH you ... that ye present your bodies a living sacrifice, holy, acceptable unto God, which is your reasonable (rational) service.*
> *And be not conformed to this world: but be ye transformed by the renewing of your mind, that ye may prove what is that good, and acceptable, and perfect, will of God* [Rom. 12:1–2].

"Paul's entreaty teaches us that men will never worship God with a sincere heart, or be roused to fear and obey Him with sufficient zeal, until they properly understand how much they are indebted to His mercy

. . . . Paul however, in order to bind us to God not by servile fear but by a voluntary and cheerful love of righteousness, attracts us by the sweetness of that grace in which our salvation consists.

"If God is properly worshipped only when we regulate all our actions according to His command, let us have done with all devised forms of worship, which He justly abominates, since He values obedience more than sacrifice. Men are pleased with their own inventions and . . . display an empty show of wisdom, but we learn what the heavenly Judge declares in opposition to this by the mouth of Paul. By calling it a *reasonable* service which God commands, he dismisses all that we attempt contrary to the rule of His Word as foolish, insipid, and rashly undertaken.

"*That ye may prove (what is that good, and acceptable, and perfect, will of God.)* We have here the purpose for which we ought to put on a new mind. It is to dismiss our own counsels and desires, and those of all men, and be attentive to the will of God alone. The knowledge of God's will is true wisdom. But if the renewal of our mind is necessary for the purpose of proving what the will of God is, it is clear from this how hostile the mind is to God.

"The world persuades itself that the works which it has devised are good. Paul exclaims that good and right are to be determined according to the commandments of God. The world is pleased with its own inventions and takes delight in them. Paul affirms that the only thing which pleases God is that which He has commanded. The world, in order to find perfection, escapes from the Word of God to new inventions. Paul holds that perfection lies in the will of God, and shows that if anyone transgresses this limit he is deluded by a false imagination," according to the insight of the renowned John Calvin.

Our minds are never free or empty. It is not possible. Some people like to claim that it is, but the mind is always occupied and subject to various influences. Normally, the mind is controlled by the world and the outlook of the world.

The difference between the person *in Christ* and the one outside Christ is that the non-Christian's mind is controlled by the world, whereas the person *in Christ* has a mind transformed and renewed by the Holy Spirit and therefore controlled by Him. The consequence of being renewed and transformed is that a person thinks in a spiritual manner, or in the Spirit of God. Paul tells the Corinthians that,

> *God hath revealed them* (the things which God hath prepared for them that love him) *unto us by his Spirit: for the Spirit searcheth all things, yea, the deep things of God. For what man knoweth the things of a man, save* (except) *the spirit of man which is in him? even so the things of God knoweth no man, but the Spirit of God* [1 Cor. 2:10–11].

The Apostle says if we are filled with the fullness of God, and if Christ dwells in our hearts, then we *have the mind of Christ* [1 Cor. 2:16]. Paul wants the followers in the way to know two things: that the teaching of the Gospel can be understood and interpreted properly only through the witnessing power of the Holy Spirit and the assurance of the Holy Spirit's witness, which is just as strong and firm as if they were touching Him.

People believe their own thoughts, but they do not know what is hidden in the hearts of others. Nothing escapes God's Spirit. Paul says the person filled with all the fullness of God is the one who thinks spiritually. The life *in Christ* changes the way a person thinks. It changes the mode and method of thinking.

How does the person *in Christ* think? He or she has a definite, positive response to Scripture. The Scripture speaks to that person. Without a renewed and transformed mind, Scripture and the Holy Spirit do not reveal truths to the person or people involved. The person *in Christ* is governed by Him and controlled by Him.

The second item to be brought under control is emotion. The person in whom the fullness of God dwells is controlled by the love of God. The best illustration of this is the life of Christ here on earth, as revealed in Scripture, as lived among His disciples, followers, and others, including His adversaries. One trait He continually exemplified and repeatedly stated was that He came into the world to glorify and please His Father, not to do His own will.

Jesus prayed in His high priestly prayer,

> *I have glorified thee on the earth:*
> *And now, O Father, glorify thou me with (alongside) thine own self, with the glory which I had with thee before the world was.*
> *I have manifested (revealed) thy name unto the men which thou gavest me . . . : thine they were, and thou gavest them (to) me; and they have kept thy word* [John 17:4–6].
>
> *For I have given unto them the words which thou gavest me, . . .*
> *I pray for them: I pray not for the world, . . .*

And all mine are thine, and thine are mine; and I am glorified in them [John 17:8–10].

When God is in control we cease to govern ourselves or to be controlled by the things of the world. The love of God comes in, while the love of self goes out. Think of what Stephen said when he was unjustly stoned to death, *Lord, lay not this sin to their charge* [Acts 7:60]. He was so filled with the love of God that he could pray for his enemies when being stoned to death.

The Apostle Paul says, *But with me it is a very small thing that I should be judged of you, or of man's judgment* (day)*: yea, I judge not mine own self* [1 Cor. 4:3]. There was a time when Paul had been sensitive to judgment and criticism. He had been willing to judge others on the surface or merely because they did not agree with him, but he did not like to be judged by the same standards. Is that not true of each of us?

Why the change in Paul? He was filled with the love of God and controlled by God. He was not concerned about what people said and thought concerning him, but he was concerned about what they thought about God and the Lord Jesus Christ. Paul wrote this to the Corinthians, who were more fascinated by outward appearances than the true and proper marks of distinction. He censored the Corinthians for seeking the approval of men, enjoying the admiration of others, being arrogant, and being blind in their judgment.

He realized that the people of God could be judged erroneously because those judging them do not understand the real meaning or true factors of what is being discussed. However, when they are being condemned, they are to respond not in a negative manner but in a positive one. They are to lift themselves up to a higher level and "to wait undaunted for God to be their judge," as John Calvin so faithfully proclaimed.

This is a lot easier to say and think than to do. Think of the prophets of the Old Testament who had to deal with unyielding and unbending people. Paul says, *Yea, I judge not mine own self* [1 Cor. 4:3]. He concludes that God is the one to judge him. He may believe he is innocent or guilty, but he knows that God is able to judge him truly and rightly. He seeks the will of God and seeks to glorify Him. It is God's prerogative to determine the value of a person and the honor he or she deserves.

The Lord Jesus says, *For I came down from heaven, not to do mine own will, but the will of him who sent me* [John 6:38]. In a very definite sense, this became true of Paul. In his farewell comments to the elders at Ephesus, he clearly states that his will is lost in the will of his Lord and Saviour.

What other attributes are true of the person filled with all the fullness of God?

He longs to be filled with the love of God. Paul says, *But the fruit of the Spirit is love* [Gal. 5:22]. This appears to be first and foremost.

He longs for righteousness. Jesus says in the Sermon on the Mount, *Blessed are they which do hunger and thirst after righteousness: for they shall be filled* [Matt. 5:6].

He longs to have the power to serve Christ and to glorify His name. *Whom we preach, warning every man, and teaching every man in all wisdom; that we may present every man perfect in Christ Jesus: Whereunto I also labor, striving according to his working, which worketh in me mightily* [Col. 1:28-29]. Paul knew what it meant to be moved by the power of God through the Holy Spirit.

He is able to overcome and eliminate a sense of want, emptiness, and insufficiency. *And whatsoever ye shall ask in my name, that will I do, that the Father may be glorified in the Son. If ye shall ask any thing in my name, I will do it* [John 14:13-14].

Being filled with all the fullness of God provides many promises, and it is from these promises that blessings flow after being filled. We are to know these things, accept them, and grasp them.

Christ came that we might be forgiven, but He was crucified, died, and rose again that we might *be filled with all the fullness of God* here and now. This is Paul's prayer. He prays that the Ephesians (and we) might know and realize these promises.

This is what being *in Christ* means. This is what a professing Christian should become. We are to pray for fullness, not for just a drop of water or a mere taste.

A poem and also a hymn, "O Lord I Would Delight in Thee," by John Ryland, a preacher in the late 1700s and early 1800s, expresses these thoughts fully.

> O Lord, I would delight in Thee
> And on Thy care depend;
> To thee in every trouble flee,
> My best, my only friend.

*When all created streams are dried
Thy fullness is the same;
May I with this be satisfied
And glory in Thy Name!*

*No good in creatures can be found
But may be found in Thee;
I must have all things and abound,
While God is God to me.*

*He that has made my heaven secure
Will here all good provide;
While Christ is rich, can I be poor?
What can I ask beside?*

*O Lord, I cast my care on Thee;
I triumph and adore,
Henceforth my great concern shall be
To love and please Thee more.*

Thanks be to God, and may we *be filled with all the fullness of God.* Amen!

19

God's Power

Now unto him that is able to do exceeding abundantly above all that we ask or think, according to the power that worketh in us, Unto him be glory in the church by Christ Jesus throughout all ages, world without end. Amen [Eph. 3:20–21].

The third chapter of Ephesians has carried us along the road called Doctrine and has taken us to a place called Love and Knowledge. It has enabled us to know better our Lord and Saviour Jesus Christ. That is God's purpose in calling Paul through His Son Jesus Christ and inspiring him to write to the Ephesians. Scripture calls us to action, Scripture wants us to know Jesus Christ, and Scripture wants us to know and experience the true love of God.

Paul strives in this chapter to take us from being mere babes *in Christ*, from what may be called "easy believism," to realizing what can happen when we become new creatures *in Christ*. Paul prays that we *might be filled with all the fullness of God*. This requires the willingness to acquire more knowledge, to pray that the Holy Spirit will abide in us, and to receive, not reject, the love of Christ.

Probably the greatest problem today among professing Christians is the lack of a true, personal knowledge of God. Yes, we have a certain amount of knowledge "about" God. We think we can exhibit a "Christian attitude" toward politics, the church, social affairs, civic responsibilities, and numerous other things. However, the real questions are: Do we know Him? Seek to know Him? Love Him? Follow Him? Obey Him? Serve Him?

Unfortunately, many people go to Worship Services, Bible Study, or Sunday School, or participate in functions merely to affirm their own conceptions of God, Jesus Christ, and the Holy Spirit. They do not seek greater knowledge, or to know God's purpose.

Paul was a unique person. He was called, he was endowed, and he was prepared. He had great theological and intellectual understanding. However, and this is important, he had a deep, personal, and experiential knowledge of Christ's love. He was able to maintain the proper balance. He knew intimately the great doctrines of faith, but he also knew and experienced the love of Christ. The knowledge Paul possessed led him to experience more abundantly the love of Christ and to know it.

That should help us to better understand and appreciate Paul's prayer on behalf of the Ephesians. There are certain factors to note about this prayer. It is rather brief: one hundred forty-eight words, eight verses, and two sentences. The basic prayer is one sentence (verses 14–19) and the doxology is another one. Note the grammar, the sequence: One beautiful, meaningful thought precedes another. The petition that precedes provides support for the one that follows; it is a powerful prayer, it is an eye-opening prayer; it leads us to none other than Jesus Christ and to the strength that is available through the power of the Holy Spirit; it proceeds from the petitions to the doxology; and it prays earnestly, *Now unto him that is able* [Eph. 3:20]. The Greek word for *able* is *dunamis*, which means "to be powerful" or "to have power."

Paul begins the concluding verses of his prayer praying *Now unto him that is able to do exceeding abundantly above all that we ask or think, according to the power that worketh in us*. Paul praises God, basically saying that what makes all this possible is the grace of God. He realizes that positive answers to the different petitions are possible only because of God's grace. Man does not deserve these blessings. They are provided only by God's grace. Therefore, Paul prays that Christ will do exceedingly abundantly, *according to the power that worketh in us*.

Earlier in this chapter, Paul revealed the immeasurable wealth *in Christ* and spoke of the unsearchable riches of Christ. His prayer contains petitions for us to realize the wealth and riches that are available.

When considering the wealth and riches available, we must be careful as to where and how we look at ourselves and our neighbors. Therefore, where must we look? We must look to God, who has promised that His power will work within us. Why? Because He has promised that His mighty power will work within us.

When looking unto Him we are to realize that He is our rich, resourceful, and reliable Father. Do you believe He has this power and is able to perform? The Eighty-first Psalm reveals truths about people then and now. The *people would not hearken, they were afraid, they lacked faith, they wallowed in unbelief, and they did not believe God* [Ps. 81:8, 10, 13]. They did not believe the promises. Why? Basically, they thought they were too good to be true, or they ignored God, or did not believe they needed Him.

What about us? What do we think of the petitions? What do we think of God's ability to fulfill them? What is our reaction to being *filled with all the fullness of God*? Are we controlled by belief or unbelief?

It is important to focus attention on the phrase *that is able to do exceeding abundantly above all that we ask or think, according to the power that worketh in us, . . .* [Eph. 3:20]. Hopefully, our petitions are the same as Paul's:

> *That he would grant you, according to the riches of his glory, to be strengthened with might by his Spirit in the inner man;*
> *That Christ may dwell in your hearts by faith; that ye being rooted and grounded in love,*
> *May be able to comprehend (understand) with all the saints . . .*
> *And to know the love of Christ, which passeth knowledge, that ye might be filled with all the fullness of God* [Eph. 3:16–19].

It is God's power that lifts every sinner from the depths of sin, redeems him, and lifts him to the highest heights *in Christ*. We need to constantly remember and realize that God not only has the power to save and to sanctify, but also the power to strengthen and to prepare us. What God begins, He finishes.

While proceeding through this prayer again and again and meditating upon the words and thoughts, are we beginning to grasp being *filled with all the fullness of God*? If we are, then we should see something of the glory and power of God. If not, then we are ignorant of the glory and power of God and ignorant of what He has purposed for us in Christ Jesus. *The apostle states that what we really need to know is the greatness of God's power.*

It may be beneficial to pause and look briefly at the first chapter of Ephesians, where Paul prays,

> *That . . . the Father of glory may give unto you the spirit of wisdom and revelation in knowledge of him:*
> *The eyes of your understanding being enlightened; that ye may know what is the hope of his calling, and what (are) the riches of the glory of his inheritance in the saints,*
> *And what is the exceeding greatness of his power to us-ward who believe, according to the working of his mighty power,*
> *Which he wrought in Christ, when he raised him from the dead, and set (seated) him at his own right hand in the heavenly places,*
> *. . .* [Eph. 1:17–20].

Chapter 2 of Ephesians stresses *the exceeding greatness of his power to us-ward that believe*. Paul uses superlative upon superlative. There is a basic reason for so doing, since our greatest superlatives are not able to describe God's power, and God's power is exceeding abundant beyond all things. It may help to consider the words of John Newton, who wrote the wonderful hymn "Amazing Grace." He also penned the following which is from the hymn, "Come Thy Soul, Thy Suit Prepare":

> *Thou art coming to a King,*
> *Large petitions with thee bring;*
> *For His grace and power are such,*
> *None can ever ask too much.*

Just think, *We cannot ask too much!*

God's power is beyond what we can think. There is a difference between what we ask and what we think. We may ask for what we believe is possible, or we may ask for something because of the emotional impact a situation is having upon us or our loved ones. Usually we put a limit upon our requests. However, there are times when we allow our minds to soar, and we dream, as the saying goes, impossible dreams.

One of the greatest failures of those who are *in Christ*, of those who are professing Christians, of those who attend worship services, is that all of us put a limit on God and His power. We want to make finite the One who is infinite. Since we are limited, we want to limit God. This was true in the Old Testament. This is true in the New Testament.

We are to be mindful of these truths and remember the angel visiting Mary and saying,

> *Fear not, Mary: for thou hast found favor with God. . . . thou shalt conceive in thy womb, and bring forth a son, and shalt call his name JESUS* [Luke 1:30–31].

> Mary asked: *How shall this be* [Luke 1:34]?
>
> The Angel said, *For with God nothing shall be impossible* [Luke 1:37].

Think of Zechariah's encounter with the angel. The angel said unto him,

> *Fear not, Zechariah: for thy prayer is heard; and thy wife Elisabeth shall bear thee a son, and thou shalt call his name John* [Luke 1:13].

The things impossible with men are possible with God.

Do not think for a minute that we are not guilty of the same thoughts as the people described in Scripture. We may be concerned about other people, but we do not pray to God about them. We may be concerned about situations, but we do not pray about them; we do not remain steadfast, persevering, or long-suffering. Cogitate about the following questions with respect to our steadfastness, perseverance, and long-suffering in going to our Father in prayer: What petitions have we asked? What petitions have we quelled within our own minds? What petitions have we been reluctant to voice? What situations that bother or disturb us have we refrained from taking to God in prayer?

While preparing this material, two thoughts kept penetrating my mind, one with which we are all familiar, the other which is personal. My reaction immediately was to share the former, but not the latter. However, the latter kept coming back and penetrating my mind, so I will share them both.

Familiar to all of us is the story of the Apollo 13 astronauts. Apollo 13 was an ill-fated space flight that had difficulty re-entering the earth's orbit. There was one rocket left to make the proper re-entry. This was further complicated by the required landing in the turbulent waters of the southwest Pacific Ocean instead of touching down normally.

The weather projections were for rough seas with 22- to 23-foot waves when Apollo 13 was to splash down, which would make rescuing the crew perilous to say the least. Millions of people around the world were aware of this serious problem and the difficulties the crew would encounter at splash-down. But they were praying for a safe landing.

Amazingly, the next day Apollo 13 splashed down into very gentle 2- to 3-foot waves making the rescue fairly simple and without fear of a mishap. The amazing power of prayer and almighty God.

On a personal note, one Friday night while living in Pittsburgh, I developed severe stomach pains. They did not subside during the night nor the next day. Therefore, Saturday afternoon my wife drove me to the hospital.

Fortunately, Dr. Goering was on duty. He ran several tests and had X-Rays taken. They revealed a large intestinal blockage. He explained and said, "We will have to operate." I responded, "Tomorrow I am being ordained as an elder in the First Presbyterian Church." He replied, "My wife is being ordained at the Shady Side Church tomorrow." Then, he paused and said, "We will monitor you during the night and perform additional tests tomorrow, but it appears we will have to operate."

My wife called Helen Wilson, the Fellowship Class Leader, and told her where I was and what the problem was. She said she would immediately have the prayer chain of approximately one hundred seventy people pray for me. Also, my wife called Bob Lamont, the minister, and told him about my situation. He said, "Don't worry, I'll see him tomorrow morning." And he joined the prayer brigade.

The next morning, Dr. Goering came in about 7:00 a.m. and ordered additional x-rays. About 9:00 a.m. he came to the room and said, "I don't believe it. There is no blockage. You can get dressed, go to church, and be ordained."

Later that morning I began the long walk down the center aisle of the First Presbyterian Church with a queasy stomach, a faltering, hesitant step, and with more than a few people having heart palpitations. However, I made it and was ordained through the power of prayer and the caring response of a loving Father.

These last two verses of Paul's prayer contain truths we should always carry with us. Listen and meditate upon how Ruth Paxson expressed it so beautifully and meaningfully,

> *Unto him*
> *That is able to do*
> *all that we ask or think*
> *above all that we ask or think*
> *abundantly above all that we ask or think*
> *Exceeding abundantly above all that we ask or think*
> *According to the power that worketh in us.*

God provides the power, and it will work within us.

In these two concluding verses of Chapter 3, Paul summarizes what he presented in the first three chapters and states that he wants us to focus on the power of God. He does not want us to doubt that power. He wants us to know what God has done, what He has done through Christ, what He has done with others, and that the same *power worketh in us*.

Paul had firsthand knowledge. During his early life, he had persecuted both Christ and the church. Then, he became a follower of Jesus Christ. How did he have the privilege of preaching and teaching the Gospel? There is only one explanation: the mighty power of God.

Nothing but the power of God could have turned this blaspheming, persecuting Pharisee into an Apostle of Jesus Christ. So you say, that is fine regarding Paul. What about us?

How do any of us come to know Christ, not to know about Him but to know Him? By the power of God that worketh in us. No one can believe the Gospel in and of himself. May we be ever mindful that it is God, not us, who quickens, reveals, abides, draws nigh, provides, and sends the Spirit to dwell within us. May we always bear in mind that we are to proceed from "All of Self, None of Thee" to "None of Self, All of Thee." The power which does these things will bring us to know *the love of Christ which passeth knowledge* and will cause us to be *filled with all the fullness of God*.

Some people ask, why do we see so little evidence of God's power? Why does it seem to be limited? The limitless power of God is limited only by the unwillingness of people to have it work, or by a lack of faith to believe that it does work. *Lord I believe, help thou mine unbelief* [Mark 9:24].

This prayer contains a tremendous light. Jesus says, *I am the light of the world: he that followeth me shall not walk in darkness, but shall have the light of life* [John 8:12]. In light of Paul's prayer and Jesus' statement, why are we satisfied to remain where we have been? Why not proceed to know the fullness of God's power?

Someone once said tersely, "You have your Bibles and your knees; use them," according to Ruth Paxson. If you will, think of it this way: The presence of God abides, the plenitude of God abounds, the power of God achieves.

Paul prays, *Unto him be glory in the church by Christ Jesus throughout all the ages, world without end. Amen.* How fitting it is to conclude this magnificent prayer with these words. The glory is to be unto Him. The church is a miracle! It is due to the presence of Jesus Christ in the power of His Spirit. That is why there is reconciliation, a change in people, and continuity.

Have you noticed the phrase throughout *all ages, world without end*? Actually, Martyn Lloyd-Jones describes it beautifully with the following illuminating words: "Unto him be glory in the church by Christ Jesus to all the generations of the ages." You cannot add to that!

> There is no age to the ages,
> *It is the age of the ages,*
> *Age upon age upon age,*
> forever and forever."

The Apostle closes his prayer with the same word we always use—*Amen*. What does it mean? The Greek word is spelled *Aunv*. It means "steadfast."

May we remain *steadfast* due to knowing the almighty power of God! *Steadfast* means "not subject to change," and "firm in belief." It implies a steady and unwavering course in love, allegiance, and conviction.

Jesus used the term *verily* quite frequently during His earthly ministry. It is exactly the same Greek word *Aunv*. It also means "so it is" and "so be it." Jesus used the term to introduce new revelations from God.

The terms *Amen* or *Verily* are used in Matthew, Mark, and John to introduce the new revelations. However, Luke uses a term that means "of a truth." This throws light on the meaning. The *Amen* is important because it reveals God's truth to us.

The individual uses *Amen* to express his belief to "let it be so." But it is more than that. It reveals God's truth. It is constant, not subject to change; it is steady and unwavering. It is steadfast.

> *Now unto him that is able to do exceeding abundantly above all*
> *we ask or think, according to the power that worketh in us,*
> *Unto him be the glory in the church by Christ Jesus throughout*
> *all ages, world without end. Amen* [Eph. 3:20-21].

"How fitting that the petitions of this prayer should glide into praise, and that not only this prayer but these chapters should close with a doxology! "Unto him"—the Master Workman who has wrought in the church through the presence of His beloved Son in the power of His mighty Spirit to make it the manifestation of His glory, both now and throughout all the ages—be praise!" Ruth Paxson appropriately concludes this portion of Ephesians with this beautiful, meaningful statement. Hallelujah, Hallelujah!

Amen!

Outline Questions

Chapter 1

Christ's Prisoner

For this cause I Paul, the prisoner of Jesus Christ for you Gentiles, . . .
[Eph. 3:1].

Why does Paul begin this section with *FOR this cause*?

What does Paul say about persecution?

What concerns Paul in this section of his letter?

What was Paul's intention?

What questions do people ask when confronted by suffering?

What approach does Paul take and suggest?

What are Paul's recommendations for responding to disappointments and sufferings?

What do Paul and Peter say about their sufferings?

Why was Paul in prison?

Why was Paul's preaching intolerable to the Jews?

What was Paul's personal objective?

Chapter 2

Grace of God

> *If ye have heard of the dispensation of the grace of God which is given me to you-ward:*
> *How that by revelation he made known unto me the Mystery (hidden truth); (as I wrote afore (before) in few words,*
> *Whereby, when ye read, ye may understand my knowledge in the mystery of Christ)*
> *Which in other ages was not made known unto the sons of men, as it is now revealed unto his holy apostles and prophets by the Spirit;*
> *That the Gentiles should be fellow heirs, and of the same body, and partakers of his promise in Christ by the gospel* [Eph. 3:2–6].

Why does Paul use personal pronouns nine times as he digresses in verses 2–13?

Why does Paul digress at this point?

How did the Gentiles become saints in God's community of believers?

Why does the Apostle present principles of the Christian faith?

How does Paul describe what was given to him by God? Why?

What is meant by the term mystery or mysteries?

How has the mystery been made clear?

What was Paul's divine command?

What does Paul say is needed for a person to receive and understand God's divine truth?

What is the primary objective of preaching and teaching?

What did Peter and John understand regarding the Gentiles?

Why does Paul use the terms *fellow heirs* and *partakers*, and what do they mean?

What other great promises have been made?

Chapter 3

The Effectual Working of His Power

> *Whereof I was made* (became) *a minister, according to the gift of the grace of God given unto me by the effectual* (effective) *working of his power.*
> *Unto me, who am less than the least of all saints, is this grace given, that I should preach among the Gentiles the unsearchable riches of Christ* [Eph. 3:7–8].

What never ceased to amaze Paul?

What is the reason for being in a right relationship with God?

What is the reason for the change in Paul?

What is meant *by the effectual* (effective) *working of his* (God's) *power?*

What are the negative and positive aspects of preaching and teaching *the unsearchable riches of Christ?*

What is meant by the word *unsearchable?*

What is to be preached and taught?

What do we receive in and from Christ?

Outline Questions

Why do we need wisdom?

Why does Paul say Christ is our sanctification?

What two gifts of God are intertwined?

Why does Paul say Christ is our redemption?

What is the Apostle Paul's greatest treasure?

What does a commitment to Christ mean?

What other riches do we receive from Christ?

What did Jesus say to the believers in Laodicia?

Chapter 4

Understanding God's Purpose

> *Unto me, who am less than the least of all saints, is this grace given, that I should preach among the Gentiles the unsearchable riches of Christ;*
>
> *And to make all men see what is the fellowship of the mystery, which from the beginning of the world hath been hid in God, who created all things by Jesus Christ:*
>
> *To the intent that now unto the principalities and powers in heavenly places might be known by the church the manifold (many-sided) wisdom of God,*
>
> *According to the eternal purpose which he purposed in Christ Jesus our Lord:*
>
> *In whom we have boldness and access with confidence by the faith of (faith in) him.*
>
> *Wherefore I desire* (ask) *that ye faint not* (not lose heart) *at my tribulations for you, which is your glory* [Eph. 3:8–13].

Why are we to deal with the inner self and one's mindset?

Why does God want to enlighten His followers?

How does God accomplish His purpose in Jesus Christ?

What is revealed through preaching?

How is God's great purpose realized?

What needs to be accomplished in order to achieve God's divine purpose?

How do we obtain a right relationship with God?

How do we become righteous before God?

What is required when God looks at us and forgives us?

What does God achieve in Christ?

What truths are we to ponder?

Chapter 5

Knowing God's Plan

> *To the intent that now unto the principalities and powers in heavenly places might be known by the church the manifold wisdom of God, . . .* [Eph. 3:10].

What were Paul's qualifications for writing his letters?

How was God's wisdom made manifest?

What does Paul reveal regarding *the manifold* (many-sided) *wisdom of God*?

Where is God's wisdom made manifest?

What do we realize when God manifests His wisdom in salvation?

For what purposes did God appoint the ministry of His Word?

What does Paul seek to reveal regarding *the manifold wisdom of God*?

How does God's wisdom become manifest?

What is significant about God's wisdom?

How does God remain just, righteous, and merciful?

What must God do to forgive sin?

How can we rediscover and recover both the confidence and enthusiasm of Paul?

What false suppositions are widely believed and espoused?

How did Paul express his faith?

What was part and parcel of Paul's faith?

Chapter 6

Bringing Us to God

> *In whom we have boldness and access with confidence by the faith of him* (faith in him).
> *Wherefore I desire* (ask) *that ye faint not* (not lose heart) *at my tribulations for you, which is your glory* [Eph. 3:12–13].

What does Paul want the "followers in the way" to realize?

What are the primary objectives of salvation?

What does Paul want us to know when encountering trials, tests, and troubles?

How is doctrine designed?

What does Paul mean when he says we are to have boldness, access, and confidence?

How does God reconcile us to Himself?

What should we know regarding God's plan of reconciliation?

How can true faith be realized and enjoyed?

What is required to move from an initial, hesitant confidence in our relationship with God to firm boldness?

What does "a leading unto" mean in Greek?

What does the word *access* mean as used by Paul?

What secured our right of access into the presence of God?

What is an essential element of prayer?

What makes possible the freedom of entry into God's presence?

Chapter 7

God's Riches and Power

> *But ye are not in the flesh, but in the Spirit, if so be that the Spirit of God dwell in you. Now if any man have not the Spirit of Christ, he is none of his.*
> *And if Christ be in you, the body is dead because of sin; but the Spirit is life because of righteousness.*
> *But if the Spirit of him that raised up Jesus from the dead dwell in you, he that raised up Christ from the dead shall also quicken* (give life to) *your mortal bodies by* (because of) *his Spirit that dwelleth in you* [Rom. 8:9–11].

What do we need to do to enter into God's presence?

How can we have confidence that God will be favorably disposed to us?

How can we truly pray to God?

What does prayer require?

What does the Apostle John bring to our attention regarding fellowship, sin, and prayer?

What does Weber say regarding a true Christian?

Outline Questions

What light does Calvin provide regarding Christ and our salvation?

What does Calvin state regarding our salvation in Christ, its doctrine, and application?

What did Paul believe regarding men and women knowing that the Gospel is so wonderful?

What did Paul believe about spiritual illumination?

What is significant regarding Paul's prayers for revelation and realization?

What should we know about the fullness of Christ?

What is the difference between *according to* and *out of* His riches?

How do we become what we are meant to be and what we know we should be?

What do we realize according to the riches and power of God?

Chapter 8

For This Cause

> *For this cause I bow my knees unto the Father of our Lord Jesus Christ,*
> *Of whom the whole family in heaven and earth is named,*
> *That he would grant you, according to the riches of his glory, to be strengthened with might by his Spirit in the inner man;*
> *That Christ may dwell in your hearts by faith; that ye, being rooted and grounded in love,*
> *May be able to comprehend (understand) with all saints what is the breadth (width), and length, and depth, and height;*
> *And to know the love of Christ, which passeth knowledge, that ye might be filled with all the fullness of God.*
> *Now unto him that is able to do exceeding abundantly above all that we ask or think, according to the power that worketh in us,*
> *Unto him be glory in the church by Christ Jesus throughout all ages, world without end. Amen* [Eph. 3:14–21].

For whom is the Apostle Paul praying?

Why should we pray?

Why does Paul pray for God's blessings and the power of the Holy Spirit?

How does Paul pray?

For what does Paul not pray?

What are the characteristics of Paul's prayer?

Why should we pray for the inner man to be strengthened?

What are we to consider regarding our intellectual and spiritual life, and the need to strengthen the inner man?

What happens when we are strengthened by the Spirit in the inner man?

Where is Christ to abide?

What is the sequence of Paul's prayer?

Where is Paul leading us?

What does Christ bring through the Spirit?

Chapter 9

Strengthening Believers

> *That he would grant you, according to the riches of his glory, to be strengthened with might by his Spirit in the inner man;*
> *That Christ may dwell in your hearts by faith; that ye, being rooted and grounded in love,*
> *May be able to comprehend (understand) with all saints what is the breadth (width), and length, and depth, and height;*
> *And to know the love of Christ, which passeth knowledge, that ye might be filled with all the fullness of God* [Eph. 3:16–19].

What are the specific items for which Paul prays?

Why are these items mind boggling?

What point needs to be emphasized?

For what does Paul pray?

What does the great Charles Spurgeon say?

Why does the inner man need to be strengthened?

What is true of a babe?

What is a reason for strengthening the inner man?

Who is the devil and what does he do?

Why do we say we need strength in order to receive Christ?

What does Scripture say about being strengthened?

What happens if we remain lazy or indolent?

What is the true purpose of teaching and learning?

How is the weakness of the inner man exhibited?

Why are we to be strengthened?

What is intellectual lethargy?

Why do our wills need to be strengthened?

How are we to be strengthened?

Chapter 10

The Spirit of Christ

That Christ may dwell in your hearts by faith [Eph. 3:17a].

Why does Paul pray that Christ may dwell in the hearts of the Ephesian followers?

What is the difference between believing in Christ and having Christ dwell within?

What does Hudson Taylor say so beautifully?

Why are we to be united with Christ?

Why and how did Paul reprimand the Corinthians?

How are we to live?

Why are we to pray in faith until we really know Christ and His *unsearchable riches*?

What is the difference between Christ doing for us and doing in us?

Why must we persist in grasping and understanding the profound and difficult statements of Scripture?

Why are we to pray for the Holy Spirit to strengthen the love of Christ within us and to strengthen our wills?

What comfort do the words of Bernard of Clairvaux's hymns offer?

How is it possible to know Christ and that He dwells within?

What should we pray for the Holy Spirit to do within us?

What faith realizes Christ dwells in one's heart?

Chapter 11

Preparing the Heart

That Christ may dwell in your hearts by faith [Eph. 3:17a].

What condition within a person shuts out God's blessings?

For what is Paul praying regarding Christ and ourselves?

What does Paul want us to experience?

Why does Paul pray for Christ to dwell in us?

How does Christ dwell in our hearts?

What is meant by faith?

Where is the possibility and reality of faith found?

What does God's faithfulness do?

What truths should be considered regarding an individual's faith?

What can we do for Christ to dwell in our hearts by faith?

What else does the phrase *by faith* mean?

How did the people in Scripture embrace the promises in faith?

What things are incompatible with having a personal relationship with Christ?

What impact does the poem by Theodore Monod have upon you?

How does Rudolph Bultman describe Paul's faith?

Chapter 12

Love and Knowledge

That Christ may dwell in your hearts by faith; that ye, being rooted and grounded in love, . . . [Eph. 3:17].

What does the phrase *That ye . . . being rooted and grounded in love, May be able to comprehend* (understand) *with all saints* mean?

Why are we to pray for a deeper and greater knowledge of Christ?

What is the initial result of Christ dwelling in our hearts?

What illustrations does the Apostle use to present a meaningful picture?

Why does the Apostle emphasize, again and again, the primacy of our love for Christ?

What does Scripture say about knowledge and love?

How does the Gospel of Christ apply to current conditions?

Why does Christ provide us with a road map?

What does the Apostle say about faith and love?

Why did God give His only begotten Son to the world?

What should be the motive for holy living?

How did Christ's love apply to Paul?

How do you describe the person who is *rooted . . . in love*?

Which hymn wondrously describes the love of Christ and our love for Him?

Chapter 13

Life's Foundation

That Christ may dwell in your hearts by faith; that ye, being rooted and grounded in love, . . . [Eph. 3:17].

What does the Greek word *agape* actually mean?

How is the love of those who are *in Christ* defined?

What does the Apostle mean by *being . . . grounded in love*?

How are we to build our spiritual foundation?

Why are we to "Take time to be holy, speak oft with thy Lord"?

What does building this foundation require?

What thoughts and expressions should be in our prayers?

What questions should we ask ourselves?

What does the life *in Christ* require and why?

Which individuals are going to receive God's blessings?

What additional insight is provided by the hymn "How Firm a Foundation"?

What can stand up to the trials, stresses, strains, and hazards of life?

Chapter 14

Receiving Fully

> *May be able to comprehend* (understand) *with all saints what is the breadth* (width), *and length, and depth, and height;*
> *And to know the love of Christ, which passeth knowledge, that ye might be filled with all the fullness of God* [Eph. 3:18–19].

What does the word *comprehend* mean?

What does the Greek word for *comprehend* mean?

What is the difference between the two?

What does the Apostle want the Ephesians to *receive fully*?

What factors are to be considered in order to *receive fully*?

What is required to *receive fully* the love of Christ and the fullness of God?

Why must you proceed from doctrine to the Person Jesus Christ?

Where should the knowledge of Christ lead us?

What does Paul say to the Philippians?

How does the hymn "More Love to Thee, O Christ" help us to understand the love of Christ?

What does the Apostle want to convey when he uses the term *with all saints*?

Why are we to accept Paul's admonition *to know the love of Christ*?

What are we to know regarding the breadth, length, depth, and height of Christ's love?

How can Christ's love be summarized?

Chapter 15

Knowing the Love of Christ

May be able to comprehend (understand) *with all saints what is the breadth* (width), *and length, and depth, and height;*
And to know the love of Christ, which passeth knowledge, that ye might be filled with all the fullness of God [Eph. 3:18–19].

Why does Paul pray that the followers will not go astray but will obtain the proper knowledge?

Why are we to apply all the truths enunciated by Paul in his prayer?

What types of knowledge are there?

Why does Paul pray for the followers to grasp the love of Christ in their minds?

For what does Paul pray regarding love in Christ's followers?

Why does the Apostle pray for all the saints to study *the love of Christ*?

What does the Greek word for *know* mean?

What are we to *know* about Christ's love?

How does the phrase *which passeth knowledge* enlighten us?

What does faith do?

Why are we to know what has been revealed?

What revelations does Edward Payson reveal?

What impact does that most beautiful hymn written by Isaac Watts have upon you?

Chapter 16

The Supreme Need

> *May be able to comprehend*(understand) *with all saints what is the breadth* (width), *and length, and depth, and height;*
> *And to know the love of Christ, which passeth knowledge, that ye might be filled with all the fullness of God* [Eph. 3:18–19].

How can we assimilate the knowledge available to us?

How can our love for Christ continue to grow and grow?

How is our faith to progress *in Christ*?

Why does the Apostle John exhort us to obedience?

Who "is the only fit critic and approver of doctrine"?

How can God's truths be sealed within us?

Where does the Apostle urge us to abide?

Why are the followers enlightened by the Holy Spirit?

How are those who are *in Christ* to strive to live?

What are the negative and positive factors in the eighteenth and nineteenth verses of this third chapter?

What did Bartimaeus do?

Why is prayer essential?

Why are we to seek the Lord Jesus Christ Himself?

How do we get to know Him?

What is the supreme need?

Where is the Lord Jesus to dwell and why?

Why are we to actively and positively know Christ's love?

Why are we to read the Word of God regularly?

Chapter 17

Filled with God's Fullness

And to know the love of Christ, which passeth knowledge, that ye might be filled with all the fullness of God [Eph. 3:19].

What is the climax to this beautiful prayer of Paul's?

What does it mean?

What is the good pleasure of our heavenly Father?

Why does Paul pray for us to be filled with the divine grace that is *in Christ*?

What is it that Paul wants us to realize by using the words *that ye* to preface the words *might be filled with all the fullness of God*?

What teachings contradict Scripture?

What is it impossible for a person to become?

What attributes of God cannot be communicated?

What are the communicable attributes of God?

How do we possess *all the fullness of God*?

When does the *fullness of God* begin to enter our hearts and minds?

What significant things does Jesus state when He says, *If a man love me . . .*?

What do the truths presented by Paul in Ephesians 4:11–19 present?

How do these truths become a reality?

What matters in our relationship with Christ?

Chapter 18

Being in Christ

And to know the love of Christ, which passeth knowledge, that ye might be filled with all the fullness of God [Eph. 3:19].

How do we experience *the fullness of God*?

Why is Paul's prayer glorious?

When desiring to do things for God and Christ, what should we do first?

Why was the statement made, "Religion seems to be part of the unexamined and largely unused background of life"?

Why should Paul's prayer be in the forefront of our minds?

What is true of the person filled with *all the fullness of God*?

What does Paul want the followers in the way to know?

How does the person who is *in Christ* think?

Why did Jesus come into the world?

For what does Jesus pray in His high priestly prayer?

What happens when God is in control?

Why could Stephen pray as he did?

What changed Paul?

For what reasons did Paul censor the Corinthians?

What else is true of the person who is *filled with all the fullness of God*?

What does being *in Christ* mean as expressed by John Ryland in his meaningful poem?

Chapter 19

God's Power

> *Now unto him that is able to do exceeding abundantly above all that we ask or think, according to the power that worketh in us, Unto him be glory in the church by Christ Jesus throughout all ages, world without end. Amen* [Eph. 3:20–21].

What does Scripture beckon us to do?

What is a great problem among professing Christians?

What is unique about Paul?

What factors should be noted regarding Paul's prayer?

Why does Paul praise God?

What controls our relationship with God, belief or unbelief?

What should illuminate our minds when we fully grasp being *filled with all the fullness of God*?

What is one of the greatest failures of professing Christians?

What evidence is presented of God's power?

How do we come to know, really know, Christ?

Why should we be satisfied to remain where we are and not proceed to know the fullness of God's power?

What does the word *Amen* mean as Paul used it to conclude his masterful prayer?

Bibliography

Barth, Markus. Ephesians 1-3. Garden City, NY: Doubleday & Company, Inc., 1974.

Calvin, John. Calvin's New Testament Commentaries. Grand Rapids, MI: William. B. Eerdmans Publishing Company, 1959, 1960, 1961, 1963, 1965, 1972, 1973.

Calvin, John. Calvin's Sermons on The Epistle to the Ephesians. Carlisle, PA: The Banner of Truth Trust, 1973.

Calvin, John. Institutes of the Christian Religion. Philadelphia, PA: The Westminster Press.

Holy Bible. The King James Study Bible. Nashville, TN: Thomas Nelson, Inc., 1988.

Lloyd-Jones, Martyn. The Unsearchable Riches of Christ. Grand Rapids, MI: Baker Book House, 1980, 1981.

Paxson, Ruth. The Wealth, Walk and Warfare of the Christian. London and Edinburgh: Oliphants, Ltd., 1941.

Presbyterian Hymnal. Louisville, KY: Westminster/John Knox Press, 1990.

Vine, W. E. Vine's Expository Dictionary of New Testament Words. McLean, VA: MacDonald Publishing Company.

Weber, Otto. Foundations of Dogmatics. Volumes 1 & 2. Grand Rapids, MI: William B. Eerdmans Publishing Company, 1981, 1983

www.ingramcontent.com/pod-product-compliance
Lightning Source LLC
Chambersburg PA
CBHW060603230426
43670CB00011B/1950